The Internet Jungle Book

The Internet Jungle Book

"Winning in the Internet Jungle".

A Practical Guide
to Internet Success and Domination

Gaia Bagirian, Boris and Ilya Goldstein

ISBN:	Hardcover	978-1-4415-5698-1
	Softcover	978-1-4415-5697-4

This book was printed in the United States of America.

To order additional copies of this book, contact:
Xlibris Corporation
1-888-795-4274
www.Xlibris.com
Orders@Xlibris.com
60594

Contents

Preface

This is an exciting time to be in the online business. Internet commerce is booming all over the world and changing for the better. There are countless opportunities to market products and services and to make money. This book is designed for anyone that does not know much about the Internet, but wants to get in on the trends and make money online. You will find examples from our own experience and our friends' helpful stories.

Foreword

When we started out in the online advertising industry, we had little idea about where and how money is made on the net. When the opportunity knocked on our door, we researched industry numbers to see what we were getting into. Well, it all sounded extremely promising. We read articles about the end of the .com slump, the ever-expanding adverting budgets, and the fun industry conferences and parties. It all sounded very exciting. "All this for tweaking a website?" we thought. But the reality was different. Online marketing is much more complicated than one might think. When done right, it is difficult and unrelenting work.

In the past, the practices of online marketing were largely a gray area because website owners were unaware of what was being done behind closed curtains once they hired a marketing firm to promote their websites. Marketers were able to charge premium prices for carrying out undemanding tasks because they "held the secrets" of online marketing. Now, businesses are more actively involved in the life of their websites because the Internet has become an important point of interaction with customers, and most importantly, a profitable point of sales. Therefore, website owners are also becoming more involved in the marketing process; they demand better results and greater transparency. Now, with the help of The Internet Jungle Book, you can understand online marketing techniques and estimate how much effort and funds you require. This book is a reference for anyone who is thinking of hiring an online marketing firm, or wants to learn how to promote a website on their own. The secrets are all here.

However, unlike other works on Internet marketing, this book goes beyond the generic bullet-pointing of a "five-step marketing success program" by explaining the Internet as a system of interaction between people. We find that far too often marketers omit the human factor in favor of the technical aspects of online marketing. This is why there are many cases where the "proper" steps had been taken to elevate a website's position, but few results showed. We forget that there are real people behind the login names and email addresses, and websites should appeal to these people, and not the faceless clicks. In the end, it is not the search engines and other lifeless entities that you are trying to impress, but real, breathing humans, which is why this book is useful even for someone who has done marketing on his or her own. It presents a system of thinking that opens up more possibilities than other cut-and-dry marketing manuals. We believe that only by understanding the whole system can one fully tap into the potential of Internet commerce. This book will also be helpful when in spelling out goals for hired marketing firms because you will know to account them for more than, say, submission to 500 search engines. This book takes you out of the microcosm of your own website and teaches you to think on a larger scale. This way, you will be able to create a website that is firmly ossified into the web for years to come.

This book teaches online survival and success by explaining the workings of the Internet as an organic system. The idea is too make the subject of online marketing less technical and dry than other books on the market. Therefore, we thought of a way to explain the online world that would be interesting and useful, an approach that would stick in your mind through providing a means to learn by association. We started to play with the idea of the Internet Jungle when one of us got a nickname, Bagheera. We were talking about some clients of our firm, and the fact that many times it was difficult to explain what we were doing for them in a way that was immediately comprehensible.

Our clients would always listen politely, but it was evident that the "Internet mumbo-jumbo" was not very interesting to them. They wanted to learn, but it was simply too boring and technical. Our clients were telling us that they often felt lost in Internet lingo, but they still wanted to be involved. This is where the idea of an Internet Jungle Book originated. We joked that we act like the characters from Rudyard Kipling's The Jungle Book, guiding our clients through the trails of the online world as Bagheera, Kaa and Baloo guided Mowgli in the book. We quickly noticed that there were a lot of parallels between the online and the real world jungle, and that the plot of The Jungle Book can be used to explain the jungle metaphor better, and also allows us to lay out our book in a form of a journey. We hope we had the right idea, and this book will be a powerful tool in attaining your online goals.

When you enter the world of the Internet, you find yourself in a place that is both nurturing and vicious. Most people are familiar with the story of Mowgli. In this great story, Mother and Father Wolf saved baby boy Mowgli from the jaws of a vicious tiger, Shere Khan. They took him into the pack, and raised him as one of their own. Once Mowgli was recognized as one of the wolves, he gained protection from the pack. Nonetheless, he was still in danger, as Shere Khan vowed to come back to kill him. On the Internet, you find yourself in a similar situation. You find protectors in the form of quality websites that give you needed information, and in quality search engines that direct you to the right spot. And your enemies are those forces that steer you from your target, i.e. pop-up ads, viruses, spam and unrelated search results. Like Mowgli, in order to be safe, you need to have the right tools and knowledge.

Mowgli went through a jungle survival training program administered by Bagheera, the panther, and Baloo, the bear. From his teachers Mowgli learned about all the creatures of the jungle, how to talk in their languages, who and how to hunt, and where. The knowledge and the skills he gained through his training became critical for his long-term survival, as he faced Shere Khan and other troubles in his jungle journey. You can consider this book as your Internet Jungle survival course. In the Internet world you need the same kind of knowledge and skills as Mowgli. You need to know your way around, you need to know how to hunt and communicate, and you need the support of your pack in order to survive.

But survival and success are two different things; the skills one needs for survival are seldom adequate for success. Typically, one needs a competitive advantage in order to succeed. For Mowgli, it was his human abilities, which allowed him to think differently and outsmart his enemies. For example, he used fire to scare off Shere Khan in their first battle. In the Internet Jungle, you also need to think outside of the box in order to stay ahead of the game. The online world has become extremely competitive as progress drives entry costs to the minimum. So now, what separates a truly successful website from the mediocre mass is the ability to bring new concepts, content and tools on a continual basis. This is especially true because nowadays it is so easy to duplicate existing ideas and websites. Internet law is still nascent, so you need to put as much effort into protecting your content as in developing it. Having the right knowledge is critical.

Success is also often associated with the ability to see "the big picture." On the Internet, this means having a vision that includes all the human and technological factors that constitute the online world. It is customary to treat all things technological as lifeless entities designed to serve their purpose until they are no longer needed. We are used to having complete control over our appliances. Of course, this theory does not hold when we think back to the trouble we had programming our office VCR (but that's another story). Anyway, the point is we usually think that technology is supposed to be predictable in its operation and output. And, if we want an appliance to give us better results, we have to either upgrade the model of the appliance or get a new one. It does not change on its own; we have to take action in order to improve it.

But the Internet is a living organism as it is in a stage of constant flux. It changes on its own with or without your personal involvement. Parts of it grow and others die out as the strongest survive and the weakest die. It changes because there are real people behind it who change it all the time. The Internet is a whole virtual world that goes through evolution similar to the real world. The survival of the fittest concept applies to the Internet just as it does to us. We know that species evolve as they adapt to fit into the environment, which is governed by general laws of nature. The universal law of nature is that everything has to be in balance.

Many of us learn this concept in school by understanding the way jungles work because the jungle is a good representation of the repetitive structure that applies to everything that exists around us, from the smallest of microorganisms to whole galaxies and beyond. The jungle consists of layers of vegetation and inhibited by millions of species. A jungle consists of layers of grass, shrubs, and trees of different sizes, and of course, an array of animals, birds and insects. The jungle is a fragile ecosystem. Everything has to adapt to the forces of balance in order to survive. All species evolve through sustaining the characteristics that have proved to be beneficial for survival and procreation. Those who fail to adapt cease to exist. It is a system of interdependence; the smallest of the organisms influence what happens to the whole system, so a change in one small ecosystem creates changes in others and the whole system changes gradually. All the species have to adapt to the changes. The system is cyclical in that changes in an ecosystem make species adapt, and as species adapt, they create more changes in the ecosystem.

Just like a multi-layered jungle, the Internet is governed by a combination of self-balancing forces. Changes in technology and changes in the world (politics, culture, commerce, etc.) affect the content of the web. Changes in the Internet's content produce more changes which in turn influence the direction of technology, development and the world. This system drives the evolution of the Internet. Because of this system, the species of the web die out and evolve much like the species of the jungle. Websites have to adapt to the demands of the market, and if they fail to adapt, new and better websites replace them. This keeps the evolution process going, and due to all the competition involved a better Internet develops. Only the best survive and procreate. The forces affecting the

Internet drive it towards equilibrium, just as the forces of the jungle drive towards equilibrium in the ecosystem.

Just like Mowgli, you need to find your niche and integrate yourself into the online jungle in order to survive and become successful. You need to understand how changes in the whole system are affecting you on every level, so you can stay ahead of the game. Keeping that in mind, let's start our jungle survival course.

You are part of the jungle

Technology — especially the Internet — has firmly rooted itself in our daily lives. The Internet has changed the way people act and think. It has become a major force in altering all aspects of human interaction and lifestyles, including the way we communicate, date, purchase, and entertain ourselves. Our communications became more impersonal and distant as we have learned to use email, which facilitates sharing information and thoughts without showing emotions. The Internet has changed dating, as we create numerous profiles in online dating surveys and exchange pictures and emails. The proliferation of the Internet in our daily lives translates into our increasing interdependence within the online jungle. There is greater and greater interconnectivity of all devices since all the hardware learned to "talk" to each other through various protocols and rules of the Internet. Now, we can connect our high-tech houses with our cars and mobile devices. You can control activity in your house without actually being at home because you can use devices remotely through the Web. For example, you can preheat an oven or turn on a microwave and cook dinner (given that, of course, you put the food inside beforehand) from work to be ready by the time you reach home.

The Internet has significantly changed the way we communicate. It has brought us simultaneously closer together and farther apart because we can now adjust the degree of how personal we want to be. For example, many people now choose to end relationships over email since it is far less emotionally draining than a face-to-face encounter. In this manner, the Internet allows us to distance ourselves from others. On the other hand, the Internet has enabled close communication across the globe with email, chat and video-conferencing. Now we are able to talk to customers in Japan at the click of a button, keep in touch with friends and family and easily find information. In any case, the Internet gives us control over how personal we want to be. For example, many people send e-cards instead of postcards. Many feel that it is nice to get a postcard because it is hand-written; you feel special because the person took the time out to write you and it is something tangible – you can keep it and cherish it. E-cards do not trigger the same kind of feeling, but despite the absence of the personal touch, at least you know the person thought about you. Nonetheless, when you get an e-card you cannot help but think that if it was not for email you wouldn't get anything at all. This is the dilemma of "high-tech verses high-touch." The Internet gives us so many options in terms of communication that by choosing a certain one you can deliberately let the person know what kind of a relationship you want to establish.

Also, in many ways the web reduces our reliance on personal interaction to gain information.

People are using the Internet as a reference more than asking their friends' opinions because the Internet is fast and convenient. For example, even if I ask my friend to recommend an Italian restaurant in Manhattan, I would still log on to check out the menu and see what other options are available closer to home. After all, even though my friends are fabulous and spend a chunk of their salaries on fancy foods and drinks, I can still get a more complete picture from the Web. The Internet proves the wisdom of the old saying that a picture is worth a thousand words. The Internet will give you a glimpse of an actual, product, place or service and empower you with all the resources related to that subject of inquiry. Needless to say, the jungle is so large that sometimes it is easier to buy a reference book or call a friend for information, but now people are so used to the Internet that they spend more time online to get the information because it wakes a certain hunting instinct: you do not want to give up until you find what you are looking for. Finding the right information gives you a sense of satisfaction and accomplishment that can even be addictive.

With the Internet, methods of conducting business have also gone through staggering changes. The Internet has made more resources available to businesses and eliminated a lot of the bottlenecks. The Internet has allowed businesses to cut out the middleman, and thus wholesale distributors perish because they no longer offer an added-value service. Corporations and government agencies now rely on secure protocols to share confidential information. Examples are countless. Most importantly, the Internet gives businesses access to a large pool of customers. With its proliferation in our everyday lives, we have learned to trust technology and have become accustomed to making purchases online. More confident shoppers are entering the online jungle every day, making it an extremely attractive market for virtually any business. At the same time, the Internet presents a great advertising medium, where the cost of client acquisition is substantially less than with traditional marketing methods. All these elements make online business a viable trend now and in the future.

Chapter 1

The Grand Ecosystem

The Internet Jungle is an enchanted forest. It is easy to be confused by all the names and abbreviations. This chapter describes what happens when you first step into the Jungle. Here you will find key definitions and explanations of how things work in the world of data.

1.1. Internet vs WWW

People see things differently according to their perceptions. Most people do not distinguish between the World Wide Web and the Internet, and use the two terms interchangeably.

However, just like any ecosystem is part of the whole Earth environment, the WWW is just a part of the Internet. Let us explain it this way: In one of our conversations with a friend from Venezuela, she complained saying that when people say America they mean the United States, "But, I am from America," she said, "Latin America." You see, the WWW is the dominant part of the Internet, just like the United States is the dominant power of the continent. Much like the US is just a part of the North American continent; the Web is the dominant part of the Internet.

The Internet was developed by the US Defense Advanced Research Agency (DARPA) in 1969 to enable faster information exchange between defense contractors and researchers. Basically, it is a set of rules that allows computers to connect and communicate with each other.

On the other hand, the World Wide Web was developed by Tim Bernes-Lee, a computer programmer working for CERN, the European Organization for Nuclear Research in 1990. He constructed an interface that allowed people to see graphics and hear sounds by clicking on a hypertext link.

You send emails through the Internet, but not through the Web. You can also use chat and swap music and graphics without using the Web. So just think of the US as the Web and America as the Internet. The Internet is the whole ecosystem of the earth, and the Web is a collection of forests and jungles of closely linked communities.

The WWW is only one aspect of E-marketing and part of Internet. The Internet delivers digital text, video, audio and graphic information to many more information-receiving appliances as Personal Computer, Cell Phone, Television, Automobile and many another devices, such as bar code scanners.

1.2. Internet Protocols

In the real jungle, the procreation of all creatures and the continuation of evolution are dependent on the transfer of energy from one being to another, as the energy travels from the bottom of the food chain to the top, and back. This continuous transfer of life-force from one creature to another is what perpetuates life.

The Internet Jungle has a life-force of its own: data.

When computers transfer data, they communicate via data lines like phone lines, cables and satellites. The method computers use to transfer information to each other is called protocol. The most important protocols are the TCP/IP (an acronym you might have seen when setting up an email account). TCP/IP allows data to be transferred as "packets," or small chunks of information. The packets are numbered and directed to the address of the receiving computer. The Internet moves the packets through various routes to avoid clogging one pathway with too much information, which allows the system to operate efficiently. On arrival, the packets are reassembled by the target computer in their original order. The whole process is facilitated by two protocols: TCP and IP. IP stands for Internet Protocol, and its function is to move the data packets from one place to another. TCP, Transmission Control Protocol, manages the flow of the packets and ensures they arrive without errors.

Other protocols are used depending on the type of data you send. For example, File Transfer Protocol (FTP) allows copying whole files from one computer to another. HTTP is Hypertext Transfer Protocol, which distributes data as hypertext, a language that gives you the ability to browse Web pages. A DNS, Domain Name System, translates domain names to IP numbers. Post Office Protocol (POP) is used when downloading messages from a server. SMTP is Simple Mail Transfer Protocol, which allows you to send messages to a mail server. Multipurpose Internet Mail Extensions (MIME) encodes data so it can be sent via email.

You can also use web-based email services, like MSN's Hotmail, which allows you to send and receive email messages using only your web browser. With web-based email, you do not need a computer of your own to use email, and you can access your mail from a computer in any part of the world. Usually these services are free of charge and offer a sufficient degree of security. However, you usually get limited storage space, so you have to delete some emails with time. Sometimes these services disallow accessing your mail with the help of e-mail programs, such as Outlook or Eudora. That is, you only can read and send mail by visiting their website and logging into your account.

Recently, however, large Internet portals started offering free online e-mail accounts with virtually unlimited storage space and many advanced functions. A good example is Gmail, the mail service offered by Google, a major search engines. In any case, it is a good idea to get a web-based email account as a backup when your regular email is down, or if you want to send a private message while at work.

You can also use mail forwarding to redirect emails wherever you want. This way you can switch ISPs (Internet Service Providers, such as AOL or MSN) without sacrificing your email address.

Other web-based email services are Yahoo! Mail and Lycos Mail.

Here's a handy reference table for all those abbreviations:

Figure 1.1. Main Internet Protocol Suites and File Formats

Layer	Protocols or Formats
Information transfer protocols	FTP, HTTP, IMAP, IRC, NNTP, POP3, SMTP, SSH, Telnet, BitTorrent , WAP
Special text markup languages	XML, RSS, Atom, HTML
Music file formats	MP3, MP3Pro, AAC (M4A,M4P), Vorbis, WMA, ASF, WAF (AIFF,CDA), ISO, SHN, FLAC, WV, APE
Compressed file formats	Zip, RAR, PAR (PAR2), yEnc, TAR, GZIP, TGZ, BZIP
Electronic book formats	CHM, TXT, RTF, HTML, LIT, DOC, PDB (PRC), PDF
Movie formats	DivX, MPEG, AVI, MOV, VCD, SVCD
Image formats	JPEG, GIF, PNG, BMP

1.3. IP addresses

Creatures of the online jungle first identify you by your scent – your IP (Internet Protocol) address, which is assigned to you when you connect to the Web. This unique Internet address allows other computers to route information to you.

Your IP address can be either *static* or *dynamic*. A static IP address assigned to your computer always stays the same, while the dynamic address changes every time you log in. Your computer at work most likely has a dynamic IP address which allows the IT staff to see if the computer is connected to the network and what it is doing.

The IP address is made up of numbers separated by dots, for example: 66.80.254.152. This is the numerical representation of the domain name **www.universalenginegroup.com**. A domain name is much easier to remember than a set of numbers (unless you are a mathematical genius or have a photographic memory), so word-based addresses are used primarily to simplify the Web experience.

Some IP nuances

If you share your IP with someone, and that person uses it for spam, then it will be blocked.

Sometimes you can hear of an "IP address banned by a search engine". This mainly refers to the situations in which search engine marketers use special software to automatically query the search engine, e.g. to analyze rankings of their website for multiple search terms. Search engines were created for humans, not for machines, and they automatically disapprove queries that produce excessive load on their servers. Search engines can find out if an IP address sends too many queries and block it for a certain period of time (usually a day). In contrary to a common belief, search engines do not ban IP addresses by diminishing any website rankings: they are simply unable to find out which websites you own because your IP address does not provide that information.

Technical bits

In the current standard protocol for the Internet, IP addresses consist of 32 "bits," which makes for 4,294,967,296 (yeah, that's over 4 *billion*) unique host interface addresses in theory. In practice, because addresses are allocated in blocks, many unused addresses are unavailable (much like unused phone numbers in a sparsely-populated area code), so that there is some pressure to extend the address range via IP version 6 which is becoming more common.

1.4. Browsers

A browser is a software program you need to visually access the web. The first browser, Mosaic, was developed by the National Center for Supercomputing Applications in the early 1990s. Today, there are many browsers available but the most popular are Microsoft's Internet Explorer and Mozilla Firefox. Internet Explorer, however, established itself as the dominant browser.

Firefox, a new browser developed by Mozilla is gaining popularity as well. It is light but packed with useful features and tools. Its "automatic updates" feature lets you get the latest browser versions and avoid attacks on browsers. Mozilla Firefox is "open source" software, which means everyone who has some programming skills can participate in improving and extending this program. A multitude of various useful extensions (and skins) created for Firefox by users from all over the world led to exponentially increasing popularity of this browser over the last couple of years.

Now Firefox and Explorer have different useful features, so you should check out both (they are free) and see which one suits you best.

Another popular browser, Opera, was developed by a Norwegian company to be light but extremely user-friendly and functional. It captured a large market share by introducing a tab feature that allows you to switch between web pages more efficiently by displaying them in tabs on a single window. This feature became so popular that other browsers developed plug-ins that add this feature to the original browser. Opera also has versions designed for cell phones and other mobile devices.

Here are the latest market share indicators for browsers. This chart displays browsers most used by Web surfers, and shows how browser popularity changed over the past year. This table was put together by HitsLink (**http://marketshare.hitslink.com**).

Figure 1.2. Top browser ranking results

Month	Internet Explorer	Firefox	Safari	Opera	Netscape	Mozilla	Other
August, 2007	79.00%	14.65%	4.71%	0.51%	0.74%	0.11%	0.28%
September, 2007	78.27%	14.99%	5.11%	0.51%	0.74%	0.10%	0.28%
October, 2007	78.36%	14.97%	5.09%	0.58%	0.66%	0.09%	0.25%
November, 2007	77.35%	16.01%	5.14%	0.65%	0.60%	0.09%	0.16%
December, 2007	76.04%	16.80%	5.59%	0.64%	0.66%	0.08%	0.19%
January, 2008	75.47%	16.98%	5.82%	0.62%	0.61%	0.32%	0.18%
February, 2008	74.88%	17.27%	5.70%	0.69%	0.68%	0.59%	0.19%
March, 2008	74.80%	17.83%	5.82%	0.69%	0.55%	0.09%	0.22%
April, 2008	74.83%	17.76%	5.81%	0.69%	0.56%	0.16%	0.19%
May, 2008	73.75%	18.41%	6.25%	0.71%	0.62%	0.08%	0.18%
June, 2008	73.01%	19.03%	6.31%	0.73%	0.67%	0.09%	0.16%

The average user tends to use Internet Explorer, since it comes preinstalled with Windows, which is still the most popular operating system[1].

1.5. HTML/XML/RSS

Most websites are written in HTML (Hyper Text Markup Language). When you point your browser to an address on the World Wide Web, it receives HTML code from that website and turns it into a pretty formatted page that you see on the screen.

W3C (World Wide Web Consortium, an Internet standards authority) also created a new format for integration of the news information on the Web named XML (eXtensible Markup Language). XML is intended

---

[1]   Version IE 7 (IE Vista) of Microsoft introduces tabs, improved work with multiple pages and support of RSS streams. Users used tabs already for a long time in alternative browsers – Mozilla Firefox (**http://www.mozilla.com/firefox/**) and Opera (**http://www.opera.com**).

not only for the organization of data exchange in W3C, but also for recognition of their semantics.

Most popular version of XML format has received name RSS that means Really Simple Syndication or Rich Site Summary. Today export of data to format RSS is carried out with the largest portals, including CNN, BBC News, Amazon, CNET News, The Register and etc. Mainly, RSS helps you stay updated on the news of the website you are interested in. Here's how it works: a website or portal, say, CNN.com, continuously exports their every piece of news into a special file (also called the RSS feed). You subscribe to this RSS feed by adding it to your RSS integrator. When you open your integrator at any time, it connects to CNN to see if there are any new news items in the feed. You can subscribe to many RSS feeds from different sites at the same time to check on fresh news from CNN, the weather forecast from Yahoo! Weather and new cookie recipes from Aunt Bonnie all in one place.

What is an "integrator", you ask, and where do I get one? Well, it's really simple.

Yahoo! and Google let you create your very own personalized space on their servers. On Yahoo! it is called "My Yahoo!" and on Google, it's the "iGoogle". By creating an account, you set up your personal home page to display up-to-date feeds from sites you like whenever you log into your personal space.

RSS allows the formation of new search systems and successful collaboration with the dynamically updated part Invisible Web. Format RSS is specially intended for the organization of information communications between people, so between communication servers are used basically for distribution of headings and summaries of news, and also to conduct network diaries (now known as blogs).

XML/RSS became especially popular since 2004 when Internet users were exposed to RSS technology.

Chapter 2

The Creatures of the Jungle

2.1. Websites and Domains

Getting to know all the creatures in the jungle is important because knowing what to expect can save you a lot of time and trouble. If you don't know who you are dealing with, you might easily find yourself cheated or lured into something you did not want. Mowgli got in trouble this way. Baloo forgot to tell him that the monkeys were not to be trusted because they had no shame or organization, and they never honored their word. Without this knowledge, Mowgli was lured away by the monkeys with the promise of being their leader. Only as they dragged him on top of the trees and carried him away did Mowgli realize he was in danger. You can get into similar trouble on the net. Shady websites, spammers and the like promise mountains of riches for little effort. Sometimes it is tempting to give in and see what happens. For example, you might see someone advertising a great deal, and go for it. You make a payment and then nothing happens. You wait, and then try to get your money back, only to find out that the company is registered in Tuvalu, and you pretty much can't do anything about it. If you had known that a *.tv* website means Tuvalu, and not television, you would have known to be more careful in the first place. This chapter lists the major entities of the Internet, what they do and how. This chapter also explains how to look for clues that identify characteristics that can be important to your business and safety.

There are many types of websites. Some are commercial while others are educational, and so on. You can usually tell what kind of an organization it belongs to by looking at the extension. ICANN currently accredits domain name registrars for the following Top Level Domains:

.aero, (restricted to certain members of the global aviation community) sponsored by Society Internationale de Telecommunications Aeronautiques SC (SITA), refers to airlines

.biz, (restricted to businesses), operated by NeuLevel, refers to any business

.com, stands for "commercial" and operated by VeriSign Global Registry Services

.coop, (restricted to cooperatives) sponsored by Dot Cooperation LLC, refers to business cooperatives

.info, operated by Afilias Limited, refers to any individual or company

.museum (restricted to museums and related persons), sponsored by the Museum Domain Management Association (MuseDoma), refers to museums

.name, (restricted to individuals), operated by Global Name Registry, refers to any individual

.net, operated by VeriSign Global Registry Services, refers to a network, like an ISP

.org, indicates a non-commercial entity, operated by Public Interest Registry, indicates a non-commercial entity

.pro, (restricted to licensed professionals) operated by RegistryPro, refers to business professionals like lawyers and doctors

Other top-level domains include:

.edu indicates an educational entity

.gov indicates a government agency

.mil refers to a US military organization

.eu refers to a Euro Union country

The quantity of top-level domains is growing and already exceeds 150. For example, each country has its own basic domain name[2], however only parts of countries protect self internet properties and demand special requirements to register local domains in the territory. See list of counties in Chapter 8 that lists countries where local presence is required for a national domain name (Figure 8.10.).

Figure 2.1. Top-level domain names

Designation	Top-Level Domain Name	Number of Hosts (millions)
.com	Commercial	75.3
.net	Networks	11.3
.org	Organizations	6.7
.info	Informational	5.0
.biz	Business	1.9

Source: Network Wizards (**http://www.zooknic.com/Domains/counts.html**), April 2008

Extensions .net and .com dominate international market, however more than 33 million domain names in foreign countries belong to local domain extensions, demanding special requirement to registration. In order to do business in local countries and be visible to local search engines you will need a local extension, like .uk – Great Britain, .ca – Canada, .au or .nz – Australia and New Zealand.

Why should I care about domain names?

If you want to do a business online, you need a domain name. A website cannot exist (and be visible across the world) without a domain name. You can get any domain name for yourself, provided it is not already occupied by someone else. The prices to register a domain name are quite affordable, ranging from 12 USD per year to free if you

---

[2]   *www.iana.org./cctld/cctld-whois.htm*

purchase it together with hosting (often but not always). It doesn't matter WHAT domain name you are registering: you could get www.google. com and www.some-of-my-strange-dreams.info at exactly the same price, provided they were both available. (Unfortunately, www.google.com is already taken.)

There are a lot of domain registration companies, but the most famous are **Register.com** and **GoDaddy.com**. These services, like any other decent domain registration service, allow you to see if a domain name is already occupied before you place an order. Furtehrmore, advanced services like GoDaddy and Register.com will even suggest some other similar and available domains if the one you ask about is already taken!

You can also find information about site ownership, registration data, etc. at several sites, as an example at **www.allwhois.com**, which allows you to look up who owns a particular domain. This way, if someone already owns the domain you want, you can contact the owner and try to buy the domain for yourself[3].

As the Web is truly worldwide, websites and email addresses outside the US include a two-letter country code from IANA, the Internet Assigned Number Authority. You can view the latest list here: **http://www.iana. org/cctld/cctld-whois.htm**. A list is also included at the end of this book. European countries have also implemented a single *.eu* code to indicate all countries of the European Union instead of retaining individual country extensions.

Some domain names have *.us* in them, even though top-level domains typically represent US entities anyway. The reason for this is that in the early days the Internet was US-centric. Country codes were added after top-level domains were set up. By the time that occurred, people within the US were so accustomed to using organizational domains that only few were willing to change. Therefore, only a small number of US organizations use *.us*, such as local schools and local government agencies.

Some country codes double as widely used English abbreviations like *.tv*, which belongs to the country Tuvalu and *.md*, which belongs to Moldova. Since the country code belongs to the country they can do whatever they want. Countries with valuable abbreviations usually sell domain names to companies around the world to generate extra income. Therefore, there are many domain names that end with country codes,

---

[3]   One of the problems is that more than 97 percent of world's dictionary is already registered as domain names, but surprisingly, many of these names are inactive! If you use services like **Who Is,** you can contact owners of inactive domains to buy the necessary domain name, but the price is likely to be higher.

but do not actually belong to the country they are supposed to represent. Some other valuable country codes are *.it* for Italy and *.to* for Tonga.

There are also second-level domain names, which appear to the right of the www. For example, *mail.verizon.net* and *news.verizon.net* both belong to the main domain *verizon.net*.

2.2. URLs

A URL, Uniform Resource Locator, is a specific text-based Web address assigned to every Web page. Every URL consists of the protocol, the domain name and the file path.

A URL includes the protocol (ex. HTTP, FTP), the domain name (or IP address), and additional path information (folder/file). On the Web, a URL may address a Web page file, image file, or any other file supported by the HTTP protocol.

Domain names tell you where you have landed. Usually, you can tell what entity is behind the website, what type of an organization it is, and sometimes the country where it originates.

For example, in **http://www.universalenginegroup.com**, *http* stands for Hypertext Transfer Protocol (a method of transferring data), which is a description of how the browser can speak to this resource and get the data; the *www* indicates a computer that provides content to any computer that connects to it; then *universalengine* is the name of the computer on which the site is stored. The *.com* part tells you what kind of an organization is behind the website you are looking at; this part of the domain name is called top-level domain.

To recap:
http:// – hypertext protocol
www – World Wide Web
universalengine – second-level domain
.com – top-level domain (in this case, a commercial organization)

2.3. Directories, Portals, Vortals

A **directory** is a database of websites organized by category. Humans perform the indexing process. It is a lengthy and intricate process, so directories' databases tend to be much smaller than those of search engines. Directories are popular for their ease of browsing and focus on a particular subject.

There are commercial and non-commercial directories. Commercial directories focus on generating profit, mainly through advertising; non-commercial directories concentrate on quality and authority, and they do not have advertisements.

Yahoo! started out as a commercial directory and then evolved into a search engine. The largest non-commercial directory is DMOZ[4] (derived from **D**irectory.**MOZ**illa), also known as the ODP (Open Directory Project). DMOZ is owned by AOL, and powers many major search engines and portal sites, including Google. It has sixteen major topics with over 600,000 categories.

There are many types of directories out there. Some directories are localized and present information related to a particular community. The trend to localize geographically appeared as more small businesses began establishing online presences. Directories are becoming electronic yellow pages where you can look up businesses in your area. Local directories create mini-sites for small businesses with pictures, hours of operation and other relevant information. Therefore, being listed in a local directory is especially beneficial for those who do not have a website.

Portals use search engines (not humans) to compile information on a particular topic or industry. They provide dynamic content like news feeds and rates in hopes that the user bookmarks the site and comes back for more information on a continuous basis.

Portals can be vertical or general; they differentiate by branding, content quality, and ultimately, number of users. This is important because user numbers drive prices for advertising space. Advertising is the main source of revenue for portals. Therefore, portals try to attract more users by offering unique tools like alert systems and messaging services. More and more portals are becoming mobile-friendly, and many also offer multilingual capability. Basically, portals try to push information to the user any way it can, through email, browser or phone.

Example: The Immigration Portal: **http://www.ilw.com**

Vertical directories are related to a particular industry. For example, some of the most popular directories for the foreign currency exchange industry are **http://www.fxstreet.com** and **http://www.forexdirectory. net**. They offer content related to the industry, like news and articles, as well as useful links.

Other directories list **webrings**, which are groups of websites with related content. Each website in a webring is linked to others by a simple

---

[4]   **www.dmoz.org**

navigation bar, allowing you to visit each website in the ring. Each webring is managed by a RingMaster or ring owner.

And lastly, some directories are compiled of other directories; they are directories of directories. A good example is **http://www.allwebdirectories.com**.

Figure 2.2. Vortal – vertical portal

Vertical portals (**Vortals**) are huge, industry-specific portals. Some of the more famous ones are **www.WebMD.com** (medical directory), **www.Findlaw.com**, **www.energycentral.com**, **http://www.omchairworld. com/pages/porter/proginfo.php** (a great Vortal for hairstylists and hair enthusiasts).

Vortals are the Internet's way of catering to consumers' focused-environment preferences. Vortals typically provide news, research and statistics, discussions, newsletters, online tools and many other services that educate users about a specific industry.

As the Web becomes a standard tool for business, vortals will join and maybe replace general portal sites like AOL and Yahoo! as common gateways into the Internet.

Vortals offer great advertising space because they provide dynamic content that makes users come back on a continual basis for new information, and they have a mass of quality consumers only interested in one subject at the time of entry, offering advertisers pre-qualified traffic. They offer personalized content to registered users, email services, etc., so they provide some grain of individual attention that users respond to.

As for example, the Forex Vortal (figure 2.2.) is centered on the foreign exchange trading industry.

2.4. Blogs

"Blogs" is short for "web log" which are diaries, or life magazines. Blogs are personal places where one can share information and opinions on a particular topic with all the visitors of this blog, and often the visitors can provide some feedback by commenting on the blog posts. The blog administrator (i.e. the person who controls blog) writes articles about the latest developments on the subject and people post replies to add their thoughts. There are some 14 million blogs, growing at a rate of 12,000 a day. Cumulatively, bloggers post content about 275,000 times per day on nearly every topic or niche imaginable. One study claims that more than 50 million people regularly read blogs.

Blogs allow you to enhance your posts with pictures and hyperlinks. Finally, a blog page is nothing but a listing of short summaries of recent posts. By clicking on any post, a visitor can view its entire content and comment it if you permit. Examples of popular blogs are BoingBoing[5] and Engadget[6].

Among the sites where you can create your own blog are Blogger.com (a Google service), livejournal.com and many others.

If you want a blog on your existing site, you can choose from a number of good blog publishing software. When selecting the one for your blog, first make a list of what you need the software to accomplish. WordPress[7], MovableType[8], and b2evolution[9] are some of the best blog software around.

WordPress makes SEO easy. It boasts a good layout and easy-to-use categories, and you can designate your preferred URL formats. It has track back moderation set up by default, so nothing is ever published without your approval.

---

[5]   http://www.boingboing.net
[6]   http://www.engadget.com
[7]   http://www.wordpress.com
[8]   http://www.movabletype.org
[9]   http://b2evolution.net

Figure 2.3. A Typical Blog Page

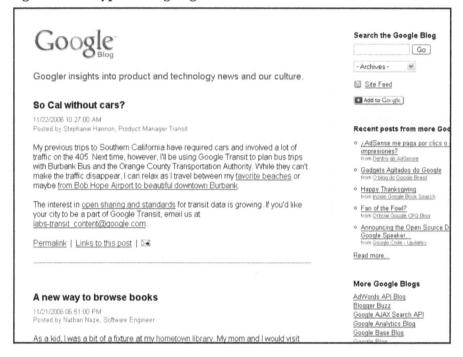

MovableType is a weblog publishing system developed by the company **Six Apart**. It features multiple weblogs, standalone content pages, asset and File Manager, user and user role management, customizable templates, tags, categories, sub-categories and multiple categories for articles, and a TrackBack feature which enables authors to keep track of who is linking, and so referring, to their articles.

b2evolution is user-friendly, but does not make SEO easy, and there are a couple of small bugs when dealing with language settings.

Traditional search engine spiders update the information between one and four times a month, and are not adapted for work with blogs. You can use Feedster (**http://blogs.feedster.com**) and Technorati (**http://www.technorati.com**) to search the blogs. Also, most blogs export their posts into RSS feeds (that we discussed here earlier), and you can easily stay updated by adding a blog's RSS feed into your integrator.

2.5. Newsgroups, Chats, Forums

Newsgroups have been extremely popular from the inception of the Internet. Usenet (User's Network) consists of user conferences where messages are distributed throughout the net in a blink of an eye through Microsoft Outlook. Just click on option "Newsgroups" to set up a newsgroup account.

Most Internet service providers offer newsgroups free with Internet service.

Figure 2.4. Most common newsgroup names

Word	Description	Typical Name
alt	Alternative topics	alt.binaries.multimedia
	Adult	alt.binary.erotica
	Photograps	alt.binaries.pictures
	CD, PC software	alt.binaries.cd.image
	Pirated software	alt.binaries.warez
biz	Bussines	biz.finance
comp	Computer Hardware/Software	comp.privace
rec	Recreational activities, games	rec.audio.misc
sci	Science-related topics	sci.space

To start accessing newsgroups, you can visit Google's group search (**http://groups.google.com**).

Instant Messengers and Chat

Unlike Usenet, where the conference itself is static, and the participants change, in chat the participants create a discussion circle, and each participant has their own circle. Another difference is that chat allows users to talk in real time.

These are the five most popular instant messaging services (this software is free to download):

- MSN Messenger **messenger.msn.com**
- ICQ **www.icq.com**
- AOL Instant Messenger (AIM) **aim.com**
- Yahoo! Messenger **messenger.yahoo.com**
- Skype **www.skype.com**

Skype is popular because it provides free long-distance phone calls to its users.

Instant Messenger is so popular with peer-to-peer operation and many people use very easy procedures to share audio and video files and can join one of many music-related chat rooms. You can use multiple instant messaging services with open source programs such as Miranda IM, **http://www.miranda-im.org**.

Forums

Forums are online communities where visitors can post and read topics of common interest. Forums are popular because they let people share information and opinions, as well as meet people and make friends.

Forums usually consist of several sections, each section overseen by a moderator, who is an expert on the particular topic. Moderators make sure that the content is relevant and appropriate.

Forums are very similar to conferences on Usenet, but they can be set up on any site. The visitor is usually registered in the forum, chooses a personal nickname or to become completely anonymous. Registration in a forum is necessary to send the message; merely reading a forum usually does not demand registration.

Forums can be centered on a particular industry or topic. Industry-specific forums are called **vertical forums**. One of the most useful forums about search marketing is the forum on **www.SearchEngineWatch.com** or **www.webmasterworld.com**, for professional web designers.

As for fun stuff, **www.Filmbug.com** offers information about movies and movie stars, and hosts forums for every topic.

Some forums require a membership fee and others are free. Some require prospective members to be referred by an existing member in order to join. In general, forums are free to join, but they offer advanced content to paid members.

2.6. Mobile Jungle Environment

Mobile phones come with many gadgets, like radio, cameras, mp3 players, and of course the Internet. Web browsing on mobile phones is becoming easier and faster as technology strives forward. We believe that mobile phones are the next frontier for reaching consumers who are searching for products and services on the go. This is an exploding global market with the worldwide number of cellular subscribers skyrocketing since the year 2000. China is the clear leader in cellular subscribers with nearly twice as many as the US. Russia has seen tremendous growth in the last few years and is likely the country with the third most cell subscribers behind the US. Rapid expansion in India will see a future climb in the rankings to a possible #2 by the year 2010. Worldwide cellular subscribers are forecasted to reach 3.2 billion by the end of 2010.

Everyday the world is becoming more and more multilingual. Although English is considered the universal language of the world, it is certainly not the most used language and, based on market statistics, most people execute tasks on their mobile phone and via the Internet using their native language.

Chapter 3

Paths and trails

3.1. Search engines

Search engines provide information collected from the Web based on your search query. There are thousands of search engines, ranging from large Meta search tools to focused local ones (discussed further later in the chapter).

A search engine is an enormous database of websites compiled by software that seeks out and indexes web content. Thousands of search engines are available on the web, and all search engines are unique. They vary in speed, size of database, advanced search features, depth of indexing, presentation and relevancy of results. Therefore, you may get dramatically different results by searching two different engines for the same exact term. Each search engine's **algorithm** (method of searching and ranking) is proprietary, so each search engine has its strengths and weaknesses.

In the recent years, the search engine world has witnessed a trend toward merging. Now some large search engines power the smaller ones.

Trail map

In the table below, there's an estimation of each search engine's share in world searches. These ratings change over time, but the general trend remains the same: there are three clear leaders that enjoy sharing nearly 90% of all Internet searches across the world. These are Google, Yahoo, and the Microsoft engine now called Live Search (formerly known as MSN). The shares of the engines following them are small enough, so the populous list of third-tier search engines — counting hundreds of portals (mainly meta-engines) — have to yield the remaining 10% share.

Figure 3.1. Worldwide SE users

Core Search Entity	Share of Searches (%)	Search Queries (MM)
Google Sites	61.5%	7,096
Yahoo! Sites	20.9%	2,416
Microsoft Sites	9.2%	1,056
Ask Network	4.3%	501
AOL LLC	4.1%	471

Source: comScore QSEARCH, Jun. 2008

How search engines work

When you execute a search through a search engine you are *not* searching through the entire content of the web. Instead, you are searching through the index of the search engine of your choice, i.e. the pages that the search engine has already looked at and stored.

The search engine is an application that searches the data and returns the results to the client. This usually means creating an HTML page in the specified format.

Most search engines search within an index, created by a SpiderBot application. To send a search to the search engine, most systems include forms. The site visitor enters their search terms in a text field, and may select appropriate settings in the form. When they click the "Search" button, the server passes that data to the search engine application.

A search engine is compiled of three major parts:

- Crawler
- Index
- Interface (query process)

A **Crawler** (or Spider) is an application that goes around the net visiting web pages, indexing information on them and following links. The crawler grabs the information and hands it to the search engine's indexers. It works like a super-high-speed browser, requesting servers for web pages and downloading them; they then send the files to the indexer.

The **index** is where all the information collected by a spider is stored. The information is logged and categorized in an enormous database. When you perform a search, you search this database, or a cache of the Internet provided by the search engine. Search engines organize content in a "**reverse index.**"

Physically, modern search engines are giant and complex computer systems. As the search engine grows, the main load is not upon the crawler or index, but upon the search mechanism: the search engine has to serve thousands of queries every minute.

To handle this problem, index is broken into parts and stored on dozens or even thousands of computers. The computers themselves, starting from 1997 (with the Inktomi search engine), are common 32-bit PCs, much like what you are using at home – yes, they have the same limitations of price and performance. The only exception is the AltaVista engine, which used powerful 64-bit systems called "Alpha" from the beginning.

But let's return to the index, this place where the jungle trails cross. What does it look like?

A search engine index does not store the information explicitly. Before getting into the index, a page goes through a number of transformations. The search engine sniffs out what words and phrases are in the document, sorts them by their frequency, weight and position each, and even what font has been used to write each of them! These data form the so-called "hitlist", and then are stored in the search engines' index database. Direct hitlists bind words to documents, i.e. they know which document contains which words. There are also inverted hitlists that are used during search: each word is bound to some documents that contain it. Along with hitlists, the search engine stores the cache, i.e. fulltext copies of web pages. The cache is stored on archive document servers.

The **search interface** is the process by which a search engine finds the most relevant results for the query. The index is searched and many factors are evaluated to determine the appropriate results. Also called a search algorithm, the search interface is different for each search engine.

Overall, a search engine first tries to determine the user's intent by looking at the words in the query. The search engine then breaks it down by keyword vectors and compares to the database to find the most related results. In most major search engines a portion of relevant calculations are stored in advance and some are calculated in real time. Each pertinent website is displayed in the results page according to the order in which the search engine had ranked them by relevancy.

When you send the query to the search engine, it first forms the list of all documents (i.e. Web pages) that are relevant to your term with the help of the inverted hitlist. Then the engine passes this list through the archive servers to find out the titles and put together the snippets for the selected documents. (Snippets are small text pieces drawn from those documents – you see them next to the links in search engines' result pages.) The search engine does its best to find out the most applicable and keyword-rich extract from each result document and use it as a snippet, to show you why this document is really relevant. Having this information, the search server builds a result page (usually of ten results at a time) and sends it back to you, the searcher.

Search engines differ in the number of pages crawled and frequency of the crawl itself. Some pages get crawled more frequently than others when they are believed to be more important and have rapidly changing information. Each search engine has periods of deep crawling and periods of shallow crawling. Crawling simply updates the cache, so it has no effect on relevancy.

Search engines also differ in how frequently they update their algorithms. Algorithm shifts can change your page's ranking, so it is important to keep track of what factors are weighed more in page rank calculations. Bigger search engines like Google update their algorithms about ten times a month, so check in once a month to see what major changes have occurred.

3.2. Major Search Engines

Google

Anywhere the search technology might go in future, Google has already engraved its name deep in the stone of history, not only as the No.1 search engine, but also the engine whose name has become a synonym for the best quality of search results.

The developers of Google owe their success to the famous PageRank algorithm that has been the first and most long lasting to reliably withstand spammers' tricks. This algorithm hasn't worsened the quality of Google's search results, and has also made made them significantly more relevant.

The key to PageRank is that it uses not the page itself to calculate its rank and importance, but the number and the quality of links that point from other pages to the given one. If we change the page in some way, we can influence how it performs in the search engines' results; instead, if the search engine looks at the links from other sites, it becomes impossible to manipulate this engine. We cannot command that someone link to us if that website doesn't belong to us. Linking to a good page is the site owner's good will. This way, Google says, only the most popular and important pages will lead the results.

This kind of approach allowed Google to quickly grasp leadership in the Internet search industry. Today, there's even a verb "to google" that means "to search something on the Internet." For example: "You want the nearest Bank of America? Google it!"

Despite Google's numerous recent offerings like personal online notebooks and calendars, it still remains a search engine at heart. Its hyper-laconic home page that contains nothing but a search form has been often imitated by many search industry leaders that tried to focus visitors' attention upon their search quality.

Main Page: www.google.com
Technology: Crawler. The main results are compiled spidering the web.
Spider (Robot) Name: Googlebot
Robot's URL: http://www.google.com/bot.html
Provides Content to: Primary: AOL Search, Netscape
Paid: AOL Search, Netscape, Teoma, AskJeeves, Iwon, Hotbot, Lycos
Submission Page: (Free) http://www.google.com/addurl.html
Submission Page: (Paid) https://adwords.google.com/select/?hl=en
Top Keywords List: www.google.com/press/zeitgeist.html
Searches File Types: HTML, PDF, PS, DOC, XLS, TXT, PPT, RTF, ASP, and WPD
Encoding: Unicode (UTF-8)

Figure 3.2. Google result page

Search:

Blog Search (http://blogsearch.google.com) – find blogs on your favorite topics
Book Search (http://books.google.com) – search the full text of books
Catalogs (http://catalogs.google.com) – search and browse mail-order catalogs
Checkout (https://checkout.google.com) – complete online purchases more
    quickly and securely
Desktop (http://desktop.google.com) – search and personalize your computer
Directory (http://www.google.com/dirhp) – browse the web by topic
Earth (http://earth.google.com) – explore the world from your PC
Finance (http://finance.google.com) – business info, news, and interactive charts
Froogle (http://froogle.google.com) – shop for items to buy online and at local stores
Images (http://images.google.com) – search for images on the web
Local (http://maps.google.com) – find local businesses and get directions
Maps (http://maps.google.com) – view maps and get directions
News (http://news.google.com) – search thousands of news stories
Scholar (http://scholar.google.com) – search scholarly papers
Video (http://video.google.com) – search TV programs and videos
Web Search (http://www.google.com/webhp) – search over billions of
    web pages

Yahoo!

Yahoo! Inc. is a leading provider of comprehensive online products and services to consumers and businesses worldwide. Yahoo! is the No. 1 Internet brand globally and the most trafficked Internet destination worldwide. Headquartered in Sunnyvale, California, Yahoo!'s global network includes 25 world properties and is available in 13 languages.

Yahoo! is one of the oldest directories in existance, yet it also has a perfect search machine. Constant innovations and new search-related services attract attention to Yahoo! not only among the Yahoo! community but far beyond. Its history has seen moments when original solutions like *Instant Search* and *Yahoo! Search Builder* pioneered the market and forced the competitors to catch up with similar developments. These features, when introduced, bring even more popularity and recognition to this renowned engine.

The quality of their search algorithm also deserves mention. Yahoo! equally divides its attention between the on-page keyword parameters and link popularity. Due to this, its search results are always relevant and free from spammers' pages or extrinsic links.

Main Page: http://search.yahoo.com
Technology: Index. Combining features of Inktomi, Fast, and AltaVista and applying a new algorithm.
Spider (Robot) Name: Slurp
Robot's URL: http://help.yahoo.com/help/us/ysearch/slurp
Submission Page: (Free) http://search.yahoo.com/info/submit.html
Submission Page: (Paid) http://searchmarketing.yahoo.com/srchsb/ssb.php (from $49 per URL)
Provides Content to: Primary: Alltheweb, Altavista, Inktomi
Paid: (through Overture) – Yahoo!, Altavista, Alltheweb, MSN
Top Keywords List: buzz.yahoo.com
Search: Web, Images, Video, Audio, Directory, Local, News, Shopping, Advertising, Answers, Job, Mobile, Shortcuts, Travel
Searches File Types : HTML, PDF, DOC, XLS, TXT, PPT and XML
Encoding: Unicode (UTF-8)

Figure 3.3. Yahoo result page

MSN search – Windows Live

If Microsoft didn't have any search engine at all, it would still remain in the history books along with the Roman Colosseum and Santa Barbara sequel. Nonetheless, Microsoft does have a search engine, and it even has entered the Big Three, although its prominence is not as secure as that of Google and Yahoo!

This engine has probably the richest history and has undergone numerous alterations through time. It started using other companies' index databases and algorithms and finished by developing its own technology. Like Yahoo!, MSN focused on creating its own community, with a super-popular mail system "HotMail," instant messenger, directory portal and more; MSN Web searches were mainly practiced within this community.

The start of Beta "search.msn.com" in 2005 has attracted the world's attention. Many functions, like customizable search settings, quick indexing of requested documents, personalized search, etc., made competitors consider developing similar features.

But the Beta was only a prelude to the great and innovative "Windows Live" search engine that was released in the second half of 2006. The range of services offered and the quality of search results win this engine a deserved place among the Big Three.

Main Page: **http://www.live.com**
Technology: Diverse. Some listings are compiled by human editors, while most results in index are provided by their own robot.
Spider (Robot) Name: msnbot
Robot's URL: **http://search.msn.com/msnbot.htm**
Submission Page: (Free) **http://search.msn.com/docs/submit.aspx**
Submission Page: (Paid) **https://adcenter.microsoft.com**
Provides Content to: None
Receives content from: Paid: Overture
Searches File Types: HTML, PDF, DOC, XLS, PPT
Encoding: Unicode (UTF-8)

Figure 3.4. Windows Live result page

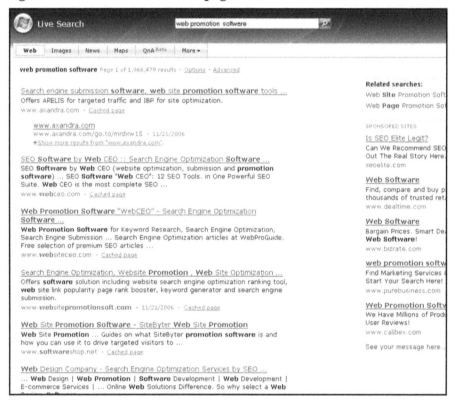

Search: Web, Images, News, Desktop, Video, Feeds, Products
Windows Live QnA (questions and answers; **http://qna.live.com**). – ask questions on any topic and get responses from the right people

Windows Live **Local** (**http://local.live.com**) – combines online mapping and local search, uses a scratch pad to take notes and allows searching around the United States in a geographical context

3.3. Local Search Engines

Local search engines serve up results according to requested geographic locations.

For example, if you want to search for a barbershop in your hometown, you can search for keywords "barbershop, town, state" and the search engine will tell you which businesses are found in that category and how far they are form where you are.

We think local search engines are great because they allow you to send results to your phone via text message. This gives users all of the information on their phone (address, phone, etc.) when they are out and about – very convenient.

An example of a local search engine would be **www.local.com**.

Local.com provides over 16 million business listings as well as a broad selection of content from websites that are geographically local to your search. The data is updated regularly and the search also incorporates information from the local web, which is contained on websites of companies that are nearby geographically. This combination provides users with a much broader range of relevant local information than traditional Yellow Pages sites. This engine frequently updates search algorithms so you receive the freshest and most relevant local content.

Local.com uses a combination of their proprietary Keyword DNA™ and geographic web indexing technologies. By combining these technologies in unique ways, this search engine provides you with relevant search results for local business, products and services, plus the extra dimension of data that appears on the local web. This can include anything from links to reviews, environmental reports, PTA meetings and much more.

The great perspective of local search engines like local.com is unquestionable. However, the monsters of Web search have already expressed their interest in this segment of the search market and are developing into it using all their huge technology potential. Soon smaller engines like local.com may not be able to compete with the giants like Google or Microsoft running **maps.google.com** and **local.live.com**, resepectively.

3.4. Metasearch Tools

Metasearch Engines use other search engines' results to form their own result pages. Although this approach seems a bit funny (why use the engine that uses Google, when we could use Google directly?), meta-engines still exist and develop and acquire new users.

Every time you type in a query at a Metasearch engine, they search a series of other search and content sites at the same time, compile their results, and display them either by source or by integrating them in a uniform manner, eliminating duplicates and re-sorting the results according to relevance. It's like using multiple search engines at the same time.

By using a Metasearch engine, you get a snapshot of the top results from a variety of search engines (including a variety of types of search engines), providing you with a broad scope of information. Metasearch engines are tolerant of imprecise search terms or inexact use of operators and tend to return fewer results, but with a greater degree of relevance. They're best used when you've got a general search because they engines return broad results. Instead of returning every possible result that contains your search term, Metasearches will return the most trusted results on the Internet. Metasearch engines also allow you to compare what kinds of results are available on different engine types (indexes, directories, pay-for-placement, etc.), or to verify that you haven't missed a great resource provided by another site, other than your favourite search engine (acting as a backup). Overall, they're a great way to save time and find exactly what you're looking for!

The primary drawback of the meta-engines is the absence of their own index database. But, surprisingly, this is their strong point as well. Their developers are free from handling the huge databases and hardware resources, and they can focus on the problems of processing the results and determining the relevance of the documents.

One more important incentive for meta-engines is the requirement to constantly invent something new in order to survive among the similar units. Like evolution in the real world, this process makes meta-engines develop some feature to distinguish itself from other specimens of the dying species and thus survive. It's not very difficult to invent an algorithm that puts other engines' results in a certain order. So, in order to be noticed, a meta-engine has to offer something above that, something unusual and useful.

Some Metasearch engines blend the results together where others keep the results separate. While they boast to bring more and better results, many fail to come up with the most relevant content. Here are some the most successful and popular Metasearch engines (according to Search Engine Watch[10]).

Dogpile (http://www.dogpile.com)

Dogpile is the most popular meta-search engine that boasts the fullest range of large engines whose results it uses. All search industry leaders are on this list. This peculiarity and the popularity remaining from early days of Web search make Dogpile the most widely used "meta."

The inspiration for Dogpile came when its founders noticed that different search engines often return different results for the very same term. The more engines they searched the more results they found.

Following this discovery, the founders set out to create a way to bring the Web's best search engines together in one place to deliver more comprehensive and relevant results.

Dogpile's founders enlisted the help of a little known virtual retriever named Arfie to help establish the Dogpile brand. In no time Arfie became the hardest working canine on the Web. Every time you enter a term to search the Web, Arfie chases down the best results from the Internet's top search engines, including Google, Yahoo! Search, MSN, Ask.com, About, MIVA, LookSmart and more.

Once the results are retrieved, the innovative Metasearch technology used by Dogpile goes to work removing duplicates and analyzing the results to help ensure the best results top the list.

With so much hard work behind each and every search, it's no wonder Dogpile is rapidly becoming the "Top Dog" of the search industry among the meta-engines.

Vivisimo (http://vivisimo.com)

Vivisimo uses Yahoo! and MSN, along with its own algorithm called "Clusty," one of the best response-clustering technologies around. The power of the proprietary ranking machine and the progressive search technology sets Vivisimo apart from other Web search engines.

Vivísimo was founded in 2000. It used a mathematical algorithm and deep linguistic knowledge to find relationships between search terms and bring them to light. Over the years, the company has built upon the original technology of document clustering with the same guiding

---

[10]   http://www.searchenginewatch.com

principle of using technology to help users conquer information overload and harness the true power of search.

Vivísimo's mission today is to help organizations find, organize and use the massive amount of information available in today's world.

For enterprises, Vivísimo's Velocity Search Platform[11] provides innovative search solutions that allow end-users to find, access, explore and manipulate all available content, regardless of location. By combining the simplicity of consumer search with the flexibility and control of enterprise software, enterprises can reap the benefits of increased user adoption and satisfaction without compromising on performance, scalability, security or the ability to configure a solution specific to its business environment. Based on a service-oriented architecture that enables rapid deployment, Velocity can be up and running in just weeks.

For consumer web searches, Vivísimo offers Clusty[12], the first full-service search site using advanced clustering technology. Clusty takes search to a new level, with dedicated search tools for the most popular search sources such as news, shopping, blogs, images and Wikipedia.

Vivísimo's search solutions are in use on corporate and governmental web sites, enterprise intranets and departments and within government intelligence agencies.

Kartoo (http://www.kartoo.com)

KartOO is a Metasearch engine that presents its results on a visual map. This search engine is a bright example of winning creativity in the conditions of harsh competition among the Metasearch engines. When it became evident that it takes much more than simply reshuffling the major engines' indexes to become an outstanding meta-engine, KartOO developed its own approach to being unique. Search results are shown through interactive Flash animations on this search engine, displaying a map of interlinked result sites.

When you click on search button, KartOO launches the query to a set of search engines, gathers the results, compiles them and represents them in a series of interactive maps through a proprietary algorithm.

As soon as you launch a search, KartOO analyses your request, questions the most relevant engines, selects the best sites and places them on a map. In this map, the found sites are organized by size, depending on their relevance. When you move the pointer over these pages, the

---

[11] **http://vivisimo.com/html/velocity**
[12] http://clusty.com

concerned keywords are illuminated and a brief description of the site appears on the left side of the screen. A series of keywords appears. You can refine your search by clicking subjects.

Mamma (http://www.mamma.com)

Created in 1996 as a master's thesis, Mamma.com helped to introduce Metasearch to the Internet as one of the first of its kind. Due to its quality results, and the benefits of Metasearch, Mamma grew rapidly through word of mouth, and quickly became an established search engine on the Internet.

Mamma.com's ranking algorithm is called rSort. It works like a voting system for search results. The search engines Mamma.com queries often return duplicate results. Instead of simply eliminating the duplicates as many Metasearch engines may do, Mamma uses this information to rank its results. Each duplicate search result is considered a 'vote' for that result. Pages with the highest number of votes go at the top of the result set. One of the big advantages of this ranking method is the double-elimination of search engine spam.

Spammers often have difficulty spamming more than one engine at the same time, as different spamming methods must be used for each search engine. Spam results tend to receive fewer votes from multiple sources. A spammer may have top ranking on one search engine, but they won't achieve it on Mamma unless they're able to spam ALL of their sources, an insurmountable task for even the best spammer.

3.5. Search Engines Go Global

Search engines now give you the capacity to create trails from all corners of the world. All major search engines like Google and Yahoo! have introduced local search capability on their search engines. This trend started in 2002 when Google and Overture entered into a battle over swift international expansion, realizing that international markets present an opportunity to increase userbases and, of course, profits.

Search engines faced major obstacles in their efforts to go global. For example, France accused Google of cultural oppression, various payment problems, and fraud, as well as language-related algorithm problems, and China required Google to obey their censorship laws.

Search results in country-specific engines are still far from great, many returning English-based results. However, search engines are improving their algorithms to skew results towards country-specific websites.

Besides, major search engines leverage their brands overseas, so user numbers are growing. The table below identifies which famous search engine has local search available in each country:

Figure 3.5. Major search engines by countries

Countries	Google	Yahoo	MSN
Arab Emirates	www.google.ae	NO	YES
Antigua and Barbuda	www.google.com.ag	NO	NO
Armenia	www.google.am	NO	NO
Argentina	www.google.com.ar	YES	YES
Austria	www.google.at	YES	YES
Australia	www.google.com.au	NO	YES
Azerbaijan	www.google.az	NO	NO
Bosnia and Herzegovina	www.google.ba	NO	NO
Belgium	www.google.be	YES	YES
Bulgaria	www.google.bg	NO	NO
Brazil	www.google.com.br	YES	YES
Canada	www.google.ca	YES	YES
Switzerland	www.google.ch	YES	YES
China	www.google.cn	YES	YES
Czech Republic	www.google.cz	YES	YES
Germany	www.google.de	YES	YES
Denmark	www.google.dk	YES	YES
Spain	www.google.es	YES	YES
Finland	www.google.fi	YES	YES
France	www.google.fr	YES	YES
Greece	www.google.gr	NO	YES
Croatia	www.google.hr	NO	NO
Ireland	www.google.ie	NO	YES
Israel	www.google.co.il	NO	NO
India	www.google.co.in	YES	YES
Íceland	www.google.is	NO	NO
Italy	www.google.it	YES	YES
Japan	www.google.co.jp	YES	YES
Korea	www.google.co.kr	YES	YES
Mexico	www.google.com.mx	YES	YES
The Netherlands	www.google.nl	YES	YES

New Zealand	**www.google.co.nz**	NO	YES
Poland	**www.google.pl**	YES	YES
Portugal	**www.google.pt**	NO	YES
Romania	**www.google.ro**	NO	NO
Russia	**www.google.ru**	YES	YES
Slovakia	**www.google.sk**	NO	YES
Turkey	**www.google.com.tr**	NO	YES
Ukraine	**www.google.com.ua**	NO	NO
UK	**www.google.co.uk**	YES	YES
USA	**www.google.com**	YES	YES

Language markets are growing with exponential speed, so consider whether your product would be attractive to foreign markets and hunt globally.

Chapter 4

Becoming King of the Jungle

Your website represents your company on the Web. Once your website is up and running, people will evaluate it and decide whether they want to come back. Search engines will evaluate it for content and decide where to place it in their search results. Little by little, your website is integrated into the rest of the Internet Jungle, the complete online ecosystem. Like in the real jungle, only the strongest survive. If your website is pleasant to use, informative and attractive, existing users will often come back, and new users will come as search engines direct them to you. Like branches of a tree, your website will grow links and become more and more deeply rooted into the Internet. It will grow in size as users ask for more content. On the Web, like in the jungle, any living organism is tested for survival, as self-regulating forces reject anything that does not fit into the grand scheme of things.

Therefore, in order to fit in and grow, your website needs to be built in harmony with the rest of the Web. This means that your website has to be *optimized* to create the best user experience possible.

4.1. Basic Website Concepts

Establish yourself. Your website must explain what your company stands for – its brand. Your website is your face and personality, so make sure it adequately represents what you promote. Generally, you want your website to be upbeat and interactive, so that people understand that they are dealing with a fast-paced, robust, dynamic company.

In today's world, having an offisical website is a must for a company that cares about its image. If properly organized, a website can serve as a corporate "business card," an advertising space and a means of branding all at the same time. Nowadays any serious business takes the process of creating its website very seriously, with the same degree of attention as other key moments of business activity. Remember, a website can either pleasantly impress your visitors (read: prospects) or scare them off by low usability, lame design or negligence, and they will project this opinion upon your company as well. With this in mind, can you entrust creating and managing a website to a junior manager just because he has time, or your nephew, a student who "already did it for his two college friends?" Like any other important task, this one should be commissioned to professionals where possible. That's why most of today's business plans include an item for web designers and/or SEOs.

Usability. Your website must be user-friendly. Website usability is a special science that aims at making navigating a website effortless. Here's some simple advice you could make use of right now:

- Get rid of unnecessary flash forms that take time to load;
- Have a site map;
- Have "back to top" tags at the bottom of pages.

Ultimately, you want users to control their experience while browsing through your website. Take a moment to look at your website through visitor's eyes and you'll quickly find things to improve.

Since most usability issues are unique for each website, you need to thoroughly analyze yours to find them out. You might want to survey your visitors, or use software that automatically tracks how they navigate through the site. For instance, HitLens inside Web CEO (**www.webceo. com**) provides a number of useful reports on the entry and exit pages, navigation paths, popular and unpopular pages, etc.

Be Dynamic. Dynamic websites are more popular than static ones, especially if you have free content on your site. You want the users to bookmark it as a great resource and then come back for more information. Therefore, update your website regularly. Give away reports and newsletters, create blogs, link resources and other information; the Jungle will love you. However, steer clear of "fake" dynamics, which can create even a worse impression, like the "news" saying that your site has moved to another hosting (no one really cares, you know) or 2001 Christmas greetings for your visitors appearing in August. Most recommended are a press release section, a segment that features expert comments and interviews, hot industry news etc. If your business or industry isn't developing that rapidly, you probably don't need a news column on your site.

Give and take. You need to receive information as much as you give away. Therefore, use RSS feeds for the most current updates on your industry, blogs for employee input, and feedback sections for user remarks.

RSS feeds are special files that you store on your site and that are automatically updated with new content, so that when someone fetches an RSS file from your site, they will always have most recent news items.

Currently, there's a great abundancy of RSS software. This solution is extremely convenient, since it both solves the problem of regularly updating your website with the burning news from industry sites (by showing the content of their RSS feeds), but also lets other sites link back to you by exporting your own RSS feeds to them. Once you have set up both RSS systems (for importing and exporting news), you let your website constanly interact with other participants of the ecosystem, without spending much time on acquiring organic partners.

Connect yourself. Linking improves ranking; your website must be link-friendly. Have a special section for partners and industry-related links with instructions on how to apply for a partnership or to link related content to your site. Ideally, you would have a special section on your site where you show other webmasters how to link to you. Give them options, starting with the HTML code of a simple text link, then banners, RSS feeds, information blocks and site snippets. When you ask someone link to you, also ask that they use your keywords as the link anchor text, because it will boost your ranking for those keywords even higher. If someone links to you with the words "click here" used as link text, it isn't very useful; you hardly want to be number one in Google for "click here". However, if there's a link out there saying "More about USB sticks" and leading to your site, search engines will understand that your site is relevant for USB sticks.

If you do this job only once, you will enjoy its fruits for a long time afterwards, since linking will happen without your direct participation. Remember to keep it easy for webmasters to use your creatives. Ideally, the only thing they should need to master is how to copy and paste.

If you have a local business (like a barbershop), make sure that your website can be found through local search options. All leading search engines allow for placing your business on their interactive maps. So, consider announcing your existence to the users of Google, Yahoo! and Microsoft local services.

You need a multilingual website if you cater to non-English speaking groups. In fact, it's a difficult task, because there's hardly anything as irritating to native speakers as slipshod use of their native language. To cope with this task well, try to find a native writer (or proofreader/editor) that is familiar with the industry you deal with.

In general, your website must be in balance with the rest of the Jungle, just like in real life you need to be in balance with your environment.

4.2. Basic Optimization

Optimizing your website means bringing it to maximum efficiency in usability and search engine visibility. It means harmonizing with the rest of the Web and tweaking your site to spur growth and popularity. Therefore, optimization is considered a marketing tool, as it creates more users, and ultimately more sales.

The process of optimization is twofold: optimization for users and optimization for search engines. When you optimize your website for users, you make it as efficient, pleasant, friendly and useful as possible. Obviously, the better the website, the more users it will have.

On the other hand, when you optimize it for search engines, you take steps to achieve better ranking. This is important because search engines are so widely used by people as their launching pad in their quest for anything on the web. **The better ranking your site has, the higher it will appear in search results. Since most people only look at the first couple of pages ranked in a search engine, higher ranking improves the chances of a person clicking on your listing, which, again, increases your chances of making a sale.**

Sounds good, right? But I have to stress that optimization is not an overnight sales miracle. It is a continuous process. You need to work on usability and visibility simultaneously because you need to test how one affects the other. Ultimately, you need to look for a balance where the processes that make your website better for users are in harmony with the processes that improve the visibility and ranking of your website.

This is where most webmasters often stuck. There are so many cases when making a website user-friendly requires the actions that are opposite to making it search engine friendly! For instance, search engines love large blocks of text, while users demand that you keep your explanations short and concise: on the web, people are much quicker to turn pages than in a regular book.

Optimizing a website means constant maneuvering between user-friendliness and relevancy in the eyes of the search engines.

Optimization brings benefits over time. However, even the smallest changes can bring huge results if you are patient. You need to test your ideas and keep track of which ones work.

4.3. Domain Names

Don't you just know when a website has the perfect name? It usually sticks in your memory because you think to yourself, Gee, what a neat way to express what this business/organization stands for! Picking the right domain name is so important because it is often the first thing that makes an impression on the user. Unlike Mowgli, whose name means Frog, you have the opportunity to pick the name of your website. And although many times the name you want has been taken, you can play around with extensions and words to find the one that is available and suitable.

There are no generic rules to choosing a domain name. Each case is individual. Mostly your choice depends on your primary goal, and your primary goal can be one of two kinds:

- Domain name as the business name;
- Domain name as an industry keyword.

Which one you select is up to you and to your business strategy. If your website is becoming a part of your brand soon, pick the first type. No one searches for Nokia by entering "cell phones" in the search engine. Without even knowing what the official site for Nokia is, we will type "nokia. com" in the address field of our browser and will be very surprised if we aren't directed to Nokia's main page. (Of course, nokia.com *will* give you what you're looking for.) If you mostly promote your brand offline, don't hesitate to choose *www.your-brand-name-here.com.*

Otherwise, for purely online businesses, having a keyword in the domain name is extremely profitable in terms of search optimization. In this case, the website isn't only a business card but also a business tool. For such websites, thorough keyword research is recommended before you choose a domain name.

A perfect solution would be to combine brand and keyword options in one domain name (if possible). Anyway, if you seriously plan becoming the King of the Jungle, consider buying as many keyword-rich and thematic domain names as possible.

If the winning idea is slow to come, you could use some "domain suggestion" tools like the one at WebProGuide (**http://www.webproguide. com/seo-tools/seo-domain-suggestion**). That tool will take your keywords, put them in various combinations to form a number of domain names, and, finally, check which of those domain names are still available.

To the user, your domain name should be *catchy, short and memorable*, so that the person can go back to your site without bookmarking or searching for it. It is difficult to generalize on this topic because there aren't any rules, but here are some pointers:

Domain names should be short, one or two words at the most. Besides being more difficult to remember, long domain names are annoying to type.

Your domain name should contain words that are easy to spell. You do not want your users to misspell your domain name, and then get taken to a competitor's site. You do not want to risk frustrating a person by making her look in the dictionary or retype the name until she gets it right. You do not want a user who has your site in mind to go to a search engine to look for you because they can't get the name right – she might get sidetracked by your competitors' sites. You do not want to alienate users by appearing snobbish. As more and more people rely on spell check to correct their grammar mistakes, it is increasingly important to pick easy words.

Once you have composed your domain name, call a friend and spell it to him or her. If he or she doesn't ask you to repeat it, you've found your domain.

Domain name should be catchy. This does not mean using jargon or industry catchphrases – those change with time, so the name of your site will sound outdated and déclassé in a few years. Instead, pick a name that has flair and meaning. It usually helps to pick a name that has repeating letters or rhyme.

Unless a brand name, a domain name has to be relevant to your business or topic.

Generally, people prefer non-dashed domain names because they are easier to type in. Dashes are ok, but they are a little annoying. A common reason for using dashes is to separate keywords in the domain name, so that search engines understand your domain name consists of several words rather than a single hardly digestible word like "yourownworkathomebu siness". Dashes are good for search engines but you have to spend hours inventing a dashed name that will also be palatable to human visitors.

Register the right extension for your site. You do not want to confuse the user about the objective of your organization. A non-profit website looks very suspicious with a .com extension; it makes you think they have a hidden agenda. Very often people will remember your name but not your extension. In this case they tend to type it in the address bar followed by a ".com" since this extension is associated with a traditional website.

Still, we recommend that you adhere to standards. If you have a network of websites, your extension is ".net"; for a non-profit it's ".org", for a commercial site it is ".com" or ".biz". If your website is a ".net" one, a workaround for the ".com prejudice" issue would be to also register a ".com" domain (that is likely to be sought first) and redirect it to your main website.

To a search engine the name of your website is part of the relevancy and ranking analysis, so if you want greater visibility for your website follow these guidelines:

Domain names must be relevant because search engines look for keywords in them. Choose a competitive keyword (say, "Web hosting"). and look at the top 10 sites that appear in search results. Their domain names will all contain the keywords.

Register the right extension. This is especially true if you want foreign traffic, because many foreign search engines do not recognize domains with a .com extension. They favor websites with the extension of search engine's home country.

Recently, it became popular to use domains that use extensions to form complete words, like **http://del.icio.us**, which spells out "delicious." We do not recommend this kind of domains unless you are sure that users will be able to remember it properly. People forget where to put the dots, and this kind of a domain name does nothing to improve your ranking. Another bad idea is to use abbreviations – most people don't really care what these mean, and forget the abbreviation before they visit for the second time.

4.4. Size

The optimum number of pages is different for every website. All I can really say is that your website must be "elegant" in size. Just as being too skinny or fat signifies sickness in the animal kingdom, a website's size is an indicator of how robust it is. Generally, as a website's size increases, content quality diminishes. However, size is a relative indicator in that it can only be measured against the same website's other versions. If you compare two different sites in size, you are comparing apples and oranges. Therefore, in order to keep your site balanced in size, you need to track which pages are being viewed the most and the least, and why. If you spot dormant pages that are hardly used, first check if they are linked properly; improper linking may be the reason they are not getting the quantity of views you expected. If the links are fine, get rid of the dead weight — trash the page. Alternatively, you can try to rewrite the content to make it more appealing, and wait to see if you get better results. If you don't, let it go. Don't feel sorry because you thought it was a pretty page, and don't keep pages just because you feel like you should have more stuff on your site. Think of how evolution works in nature: every creature only keeps features that are important for survival and procreation while other features disappear with new generations. In the same manner, your website should only keep features that have been proven to be useful to your users and profitable to you in some way. Nonetheless, from the SEO (search engine optimization) point of view, the more pages, the more indexable content, the better for the search engines.

When you create your next page remember that it is one more candidate to appear in the search results, thus a potential traffic generator. Each page of the site — not only the home page — should be created with search engines in mind.

Like everything in the Jungle, this is a matter of balance. Once you feel that your visitors might be interested in some new content, don't hesitate to put it on your site. As soon as you've approved adding another page, remember that it must fit well into the existing structure, be relevant for the site theme and contain its own unique keywords for the search engines.

4.5. Color

In the Internet Jungle, color is a tricky subject because every person has their own perception of what each color represents, formed by observing traditional connotations and individual experiences. Everyone has a unique taste in color. Therefore, it helps to think of color the way animals do. To them, color is a means to an end. They use color to camouflage themselves in the event of danger, to attract the opposite sex for mating, and to attract prey while hunting. To many, appearance is critical for survival and procreation. Treat your website's color as if it was your fur. Ask yourself, what is the function of the color? Is it a means to attract a specific group to your website, or to communicate your corporate identity? What do you want the colors to represent? Should they demonstrate that you are serious, or that you are hip and trendy? Will they suggest that you are scientific, or corporate, or something else entirely? List a number of qualities that you consider your company to have, and then prioritize according to what you deem most important. Pick the things that represent your company, and then think of the colors that fit your image and serve the purpose at hand. Here are some general suggestions applicable to color selection:

Color should be brilliant but not to the point of irritation.

Color represents how serious you want to appear. To most people bright colors are associated with being playful and fresh and darker colors are associated with seriousness. Selecting bright colors for a traditionally conservative business often sends a message that you want to put a new spin on things and relate to younger generations.

Color is more important in multicultural sites because it is far more difficult to generalize on the global level. The way people perceive any color in different cultures varies from one nation to another. Therefore, you have to be extra careful and conduct extensive advanced research before you select the colors for a multilingual website. Please refer to Chapter 8, The Global Jungle for more information on the connotation of color in different cultures.

4.6. Usability

Usability can make or break your website. It is so important because it is one of the principal determining factors of whether a user will come back. Consider it an intricate part of your Jungle hunting skills, because good usability allows you to get the user closer to the point of sale.

Now, you might consider adding an innovative navigation bar or other gimmicks and high-tech elements to your site to impress users. While there are many reasons to watch for up-and-coming usability options, the golden rule is to make your website's features as familiar as possible to any user. This means applying standards when possible. Nobody wants to learn a whole new navigation system just to look at one site; you want the user to be able to recognize how to use it right away without thinking because you want them to think of the purchase they are going to make, and nothing else. You should aim at creating a familiar user experience, not a new one. Think of Mowgli. He assimilated into the Jungle and truly became a part of his wolf family because he learned how to behave and interact with creatures of the jungle in a way that is understandable and familiar to them. Let the others push new standards while you make money. Once the new standards are widely accepted, create a version of your website with the new elements.

It is surprising how often you meet a bulky heap of JavaScript/CSS tricks on the websites of unexperienced webmasters (college students, personal home pages, etc). These people always learn cutting-edge technology and are eager to apply this knowledge all in one place just because it's interesting and innovative. On the contrary, the most prominent and famous sites keep it simple, and this is their advantage: **websites are created for humans; humans are not created for websites**.

Most importantly, remember that good usability means that a user should be able to find the needed information easily. You need to guide people through the site to the right page to convert clicks into sales. The better your website's usability, the more chances you have to trap your prey.

Here are some key usability concepts:

Allow users to control the experience. When building your site, bear in mind that different people view your site with different means. Some use computers, some PDA's, and still others have it read to them. Therefore, you have to pay attention to text size and page width. It is better to set text size or pallet size to relative, not exact values, because it will adjust according to the size of the window. Page width should be set using percentages, so that it adjusts to fit the size of the screen. This way, PDA users can view your pages on their small screens.

Do not place excessive text inside images. Text can be difficult to read and too large when viewed from a PDA or a different platform than it was designed for. Search engines do not scan images so the text inside the images will have no affect on your site's ranking.

Keep a consistent site design. At this point, Internet surfers are used to having certain things in certain places. For example, people are used to seeing the company name and logo on the top of the page. There is usually a link to the home page in either top corner. Basically, you should aim to make the user comfortable when visiting your site. This means that you should follow the rules set by the traditions of the Internet, even if you have some great new ideas. You need to be consistent throughout the site.

Have clear navigation. You need to include a search box if you have a lot of content on your site. Remember that the Internet was developed as a tool for exchanging information, so people are still used to the idea that the Internet should provide free content. Therefore, if you have lots of useful content, users will want to have good tools that make information easy to find. Some search engines like Freefind and Atomz offer to build in-site level search into any website. However, you do not need a site level search if you have a relatively small site. A site map is adequate to make the user's experience pleasurable.

Use alternative text tags with images. Nowadays all browsers can display images, and there are no problems to downloading them over the broadband connection. So why supply any additional description, you ask? Well, search engines don't recognize the content of images yet. By reading its alternative description, a search engine can bind your image to some keywords and show it in the "image search" results.

Use standards where applicable. Certain Internet practices have become standard; for example, everyone knows that a blue underline represents a hyperlink. People are used to having a navigation bar at the top or on the left column.

Keep file sizes small. If your page is too big, it will load slowly and the user will most likely abandon it. Bear in mind that people use different Internet connections, so download speeds vary significantly. This becomes especially important when you are dealing with multilingual sites because every country differs in how advanced their Internet connection is.

Have search or a link to site level search on every page. On smaller sites a link to a site map will work better than site level search because a site search is not likely to return adequate results.

4.7. Content

Every trade has its golden rules that are above discussion. One of the rules for search engine optimization is "Content is King." Surprisingly, it is so often overlooked.

Philip Kotler, a marketing guru, once said, "The aim of marketing is to make marketing unnecessary". This statement mirrors our opinion about content-rich websites: the goal is to create a site that does not need optimization. If your website is interesting to the visitors, if it contains quality and unique texts that are regularly updated, your site does all optimization work for you. Other webmasters will enjoy linking to you. People will quote you and send your information by e-mail to their friends. Search engines will put you high up in the result pages for relevant keywords.

The conclusion? Content is indispensable in creating a successful site.

In the online Jungle, content represents your personality and health. No one wants to make friends with a dull person. Therefore, your website's content should be engaging and fun. It should also be easy to read and understand. When you write your website, try to present information as if you are having a *conversation* with the visitor. This puts people at ease because they can see that there are real people behind the website.

No one wants to do business with a weak company. Your content shows how healthy your website is, so you need to show everyone how robust your health is by taking care of all your organs – all your web pages.

Your content should also be *original*. Sure, you can include articles and references, but original content makes you unique. Someone who is looking for information does not want to read the same thing on your website as they've seen on the previous one. When it comes to SEO, unique content solely decides whether you win or lose: search engines may weed out your brilliant-looking pages as duplicates to something they've already seen, so you will never get search traffic.

Even websites that just sell products need quality content. Only a small number of people start searching with a particular product in mind. Having good content will attract those who are looking for a solution for some kind of problem or need, but do not know which particular product they need. Therefore, even for product sites, having good content is crucial for converting users into buyers.

Writing specifically for your *target audience* is the single most important concept in creating good content. Think about who you want to visit your site and why, and then think of the specific topics that would be interesting to this group.

Also, check the spelling. Having misspelled words on your website will make it appear sloppy and your company will come off as unprofessional. It makes users think that the people behind the website are a bunch of slobs and that they did not even take the time to make the website appealing or clean.

Once upon a time optimization for misspellings was popular. Webmasters created special pages optimized for the misspelled words. People who made mistakes typing their search terms found exactly these pages, thus a website was able to escape competition for this small share of searchers.

This idea isn't really good, because today search engines will always suggest the correct variant ("did you mean: . . .") and those who entered a search with a typo will mostly use this link before even looking at the search results. Also, remember that you sacrifice the image of your company for the sake of a doubtful search traffic bonus.

4.8. Keywords

Keywords are search terms that you think people are using to look for information related to your products and services on your website. When someone makes a query, search engines evaluate your website's relevancy by looking at whether requested search terms are present, and they serve up results according to each website's ranking for the term searched. Therefore, you can think of keywords as bait, in that they attract potential clients to your website.

In order to take advantage of this system, you need to optimize your website by adding your keywords in the appropriate places. Each search engine's algorithm is different, but generally, they look at the website's *title tags, headings,* and **body text** to determine where to rank your site in their results. That's where you should add your keywords.

Before you start adjusting your website's tags and text, you need to choose appropriate keywords. Good keywords are juicy bait for your customers, so take your time to select the most powerful ones.

Keyword selection has no rules. It is an art rather than a science. Even the most experienced webmaster can make a bad guess. Selecting keywords is a balancing act because the terms should be targeted enough to attract the right kind of traffic, but general enough to include all prospective customers. A search term must be popular enough, on one hand, so that there are a significant number of people that use it in the search engines; on the other hand, it mustn't have fierce competition, or you will have a hard time pushing your site high in the search results.

So, when selecting keywords, you need to have the target audience, the competition, and search engines in mind.

Start by reading the home page. Then ask yourself, what is the main idea? What are you trying to tell the reader? Which sentences best describe what you are trying to communicate? Which terms are the most precise? Then think of the search terms people might use to look for that particular page. Make a list of the terms that came to your mind. Repeat this process and make a list for each page of your website. The keywords on these lists should overlap somewhat, but should distinctly cover different areas. This way, you can optimize each page for certain keywords and try to get good ranking for many terms.

Once you have your keywords ready, check them for search popularity. You can use various freely available **keyword suggestion tools** to see how many times each keyword or phrase was searched over a period of time. Several paid services such as WordTracker[13] are also available.

Most often, you will come across data on "daily searches" and "monthly searches".

Nowadays, the main goal of keyword research is to find the best balance between keyword popularity and its competition. Popularity

---

[13]   **http://www.wordtracker.com**

means how many people search for a keyword, and competition means how many websites already appear high in the search results for this keyword. The sites that occupy the top 10 or 20 positions (first two pages of search results) are keyword leaders. It is also useful to know how strong the leaders are. If no one of them is optimized for your term, and they won leadership by accident, your way to the #1 position will be easy. If the competitors are strong and highly relevant for the chosen term, you might consider switching to another one.

The tools you can use to find keyword suggestion usually also offer some kind of keyword estimation. At least they tell you how often a word has been searched throughout the previous month and how many people who search for keywords click on the sponsored ads (Google AdWords Keyword Tool[14]).

The above mentioned tools belong to search engines themselves. There are also independent software solutions (Like WordTracker or Web CEO Keywords Tool). None of the tools will ever give you an accurate estimation of how often people really search the given phrase throughout the world because the largest players like Google are not interested in publishing these figures. Still, you can use several tools to control and correct each other.

While it is difficult derive an exact number of the daily searches (i.e. the demand) for a keyword, another parameter – competition, i.e. the supply – is easily analyzed using a broad range of indicators.

Competition is defined by how many sites are found in a particular search engine for a search terms, how many of them are really focused on this term and how strong the leaders are.

Knowing your competition helps you choose the best strategy: whether to target several highly relevant phrases, or a larger number of less popular and less relevant terms.

Daily searches and competition are used to find out the KEI (Keyword Effectiveness Index) for each keyword to facilitate your choice. Keywords with higher demand and lower competition will have the higher KEI, so sorting a list of keywords by KEI helps you pinpoint the best suggestions. You can find the KEI calculation in some advanced keyword tools, like Web CEO and WordTracker.

Such an analysis is the keystone of all optimization process. Target the right keywords, and watch your sales grow. Target the wrong keywords, and see your business lag behind the competition.

---

[14]   https://adwords.google.com/select/TrafficEstimatorSandbox

Let's summarize the above process in several steps:

- Spot the words and phrases that best describe your business;
- Enter these in keyword suggestion tools, to find out what people *really* search on that topic;
- Make up a list of keywords that contains daily (or monthly) searches and competition figures for each keyword / phrase;
- Calculate the KEI for each key phrase. The keywords with the highest KEI are the best to optimize for.

In our opinion, one of the best programs for keyword research is Web CEO. It's a paid software, which nonetheless has a free edition that you don't have to pay for and that has no time limitations (no trial period). The free edition lets you enter a word or phrase and get up to five real-world search suggestions, with daily searches and KEI for each, and get a quick snapshot of the competition. In the paid version, 1,000 suggestions and advanced competition analysis are available.

Your research should tell you which keywords from your lists are the least popular and should be dropped. Look at the keywords that are the most popular, and eliminate the terms that are very broad, like "free," "download music," etc. This might seem illogical at first.

However, such terms are usually highly competitive and offer little chance to leverage your advertising dollars against the big guys. What good does it have if you rank 500th for "free?" No one is going to look through hundreds of results to find you. The best approach is to combine general terms with those unique to your business.

After the initial elimination, narrow down each list to one or two medium-popular keywords that you think will be most effective. You should concentrate on optimizing each page only for those keywords that are left on each list. This might also go against logic.

You should optimize your pages for *keyword density*. Do not put all your eggs in one basket. Each page should be optimized for only several keywords because as you add more keywords to the mix, your page becomes less focused as you dilute the keyword density. The result will be that the text on your page will sound machine-generated and will bore and scare off potential customers.

It is a good idea to optimize the same page for keyword phrases that include *shared keywords*. Your keyword phrases should overlap. So, if you do a good job, your page should rank well for your subject and closely related subjects at the same time.

Some Common Keyword Nuances

How long should the search terms be? You have to think about phrases as much as single keywords. The debate on term length has not been settled. Some say that those who search longer terms constitute better-targeted traffic. Others say that concise search terms mean better conversion. From our experience we can say that good keyword phrases are between two and five words long.

Based on Internet statistics provider OneStat.com, queries using two keywords are used the most. The second most popular are queries using one word. Three keyword searches are third in popularity.

- 2-keyword search – 32.58%
- 1-keyword search – 25.61%
- 3-keyword search – 19.02%
- 4-keyword search – 12.83%

Hyphenated keywords. Most search engines treat hyphens as a space. Therefore, if you search for buzz-word and buzzword you will find two separate results. So, when choosing which keyword to use, look at which version is used more frequently.

Keywords with multiple meanings. Some words have different meanings depending on the context. If you run into this problem, try to come up with keyword phrases that put the word in context. Puns should almost always be avoided to qualify your traffic.

Generic words. Many people optimize their websites for generic words because they think it will bring a lot of traffic. While this is true, getting good page rank through optimizing for generic keywords is complicated because of fierce competition. And even if you do a great job at that, you will receive general traffic that will not convert at the website. Targeted traffic is always better.

Abbreviations. Optimizing for abbreviations might help you bring some targeted users because generally only those that are very comfortable with the term will use it to search for something. However, most people type in the whole word or phrase. Generally, I do not recommend focusing on abbreviated keywords, but use them occasionally.

Slang and catch phrases. Slang and catch phrases come and go. While optimizing for such words may help bring targeted traffic and cut competition, you need to watch for when the terms become outdated and change your website accordingly. But once you change the keywords, you will have to optimize for the regular keywords. Therefore, it is best to optimize for regular keywords from the start, and use slang keywords in pay-per-click for the time these buzz words are hot.

How to Find the Right Keywords: the Practice

Advanced keyword suggestion tools not only give you suggestions, but will help you analyze them and pick out the best choices for your site. We will illustrate this with the example of **Web CEO Keyword Suggestion Tool** that offers an advanced analysis of keyword popularity and competition.

Web CEO works with keywords in four tabs. On the first tab, you enter a generic term like "weather forecast" and see what words are used by your competition to promote themselves (Web CEO finds the competition by querying the search engines for "weather forecast," looking at the result pages and analyzing the leaders' pages). This tab gives you insight on other words related to your topic.

On the second tab, you enter the same or more specific term, and see what people really search for in the engines. For instance you may enter "weather forecast" and end up with a list of words like "Texas weather forecast," "long-range weather forecast," "weather forecast software," etc. Each word will have the number of daily searches and competition attached to it, and KEI is automatically calculated. Here you can pick out some keywords that seem appropriate to you and put them into a "basket."

Figure 4.1. Keyword research in Web CEO

Web CEO - [Keywords :: www.websiteceo.com/ :: http://www.websiteceo.com/]
File Features View Windows Account Help — Project www.websiteceo.com/
1. Get suggestions | 2. Research keywords | 3. View competitors | 4. Analyze competition — Teach Me

Enter your keyword or phrase — Keyword basket

Keywords: optimization — Exact match — Add from file — Basket: General basket

No.	Keyword/phrase	Daily World Searches	Competition	KEI
1	search engine optimization	74 071	106 000 000	51.760
2	search engine optimization company	3 762	191 000 000	0.074
3	search engine optimization services	2 884	82 100 000	0.101
4	search engine optimization firm	2 827	191 000 000	0.042
5	optimization	2 099	132 000 000	0.033
6	web site optimization	1 818	366 000 000	0.009
7	search engine optimization specialist	1 706	6 980 000	0.417
8	cyprus search engine optimization	1 594	1 740 000	1.460
9	website optimization	1 583	104 000 000	0.024
10	search engine optimization service	1 456	68 900 000	0.031
11	web site optimization services	1 434	51 900 000	0.040
12	seo optimization	1 246	27 400 000	0.057
13	engine optimization	1 239	89 200 000	0.017
14	meta tag optimization	1 059	3 540 000	0.317
15	website optimization firm	964	31 100 000	0.030
16	search engine optimization training	919	19 300 000	0.044
17	web site optimization service	862	116 000 000	0.006
18	search engine optimization software	809	33 200 000	0.020
19	optimization services	748	122 000 000	0.005
20	meta optimization	713	11 800 000	0.043
21	engine optimization search	698	87 100 000	0.006
22	site optimization	666	60 900 000	0.005
23	optimization software optimization s..	608	127 000 000	0.003
24	search and engine and optimization	605	79 300 000	0.005
25	meta optimization service	585	9 390 000	0.036

Add →

No.	Keyword/phrase	Daily World Searches	Competition	KEI
1	search engine optimiz..	74 071	106 000 000	51.760
2	search engine optimiz..	3 762	191 000 000	0.074
3	search engine optimiz..	2 884	82 100 000	0.101
4	search engine optimiz..	2 827	191 000 000	0.042
5	optimization	2 099	132 000 000	0.033
6	web site optimization	1 818	366 000 000	0.009
7	search engine optimiz..	1 706	6 980 000	0.417
8	cyprus search engine..	1 594	1 740 000	1.460
9	website optimization	1 583	104 000 000	0.024
10	search engine optimiz..	1 456	68 900 000	0.031
11	web site optimization..	1 434	51 900 000	0.040
12	seo optimization	1 246	27 400 000	0.057
13	engine optimization	1 239	89 200 000	0.017
14	meta tag optimization	1 059	3 540 000	0.317
15	website optimization fi..	964	31 100 000	0.030
16	search engine optimiz..	919	19 300 000	0.044
17	web site optimization..	862	116 000 000	0.006
18	search engine optimiz..	809	33 200 000	0.020
19	optimization services	748	122 000 000	0.005
20	meta optimization	713	11 800 000	0.043
21	engine optimization s..	698	87 100 000	0.006

Notes
type your notes on the basket here

On the third tab, you pick a word from your basket and get a quick overview of the keyword leaders, along with their Google PageRank indication (this helps you measure leaders' strength and decide whether to leave the word in the basket or to discard it because of the harsh competition). We will explain PageRank in the further chapters and explain why it matters.

Finally, tab four (available in the paid version only) helps you research competition more thoroughly and estimate which key phrases are worth fighting for. It displays PageRanks, traffic that leaders currently receive, leaders' link popularity and other values that help you make the decision.

Figure 4.2. Keyword competition analysis by Web CEO

Keywords	Daily World Searches	KEI	Pages with keyword	Titles with keyword	Links to #1	Links to #2	Traffic Rank for #1	Traffic Rank for #2	Bid #1	Bid #2
search engine optimization	74 071	51 760	57 700 000	787 000	7 110	420	2 323	14	3.01	2.00
search engine optimization company	3 762	0.074	98 600 000	47 700	1 430	145	140 702	399 311	2.25	1.60
search engine optimization services	2 984	0.101	141 000 000	81 600	7 110	428	2 323	50 637	5.00	2.11
search engine optimization firm	2 827	0.042	23 300 000	15 200	813	579	40 717	33 887	2.01	2.00
optimization	2 099	0.033	95 400 000	5 120 000	848	65	660 231	13 509	5.00	1.50
web site optimization	1 818	0.009	84 100 000	66 400	702	376	6 064	6 064	2.02	2.02
search engine optimization specialist	1 706	0.417	1 350 000	699	3	587	74 608	22 078	3.91	3.11
cyprus search engine optimization	1 594	1.460	1 090 000	123	·	3	2 430 694	·	0.20	0.15
website optimization	1 583	0.024	43 700 000	112 000	702	376	6 064	6 064	2.02	2.02
search engine optimization service	1 456	0.031	42 500 000	13 900	7 110	428	2 323	50 637	n/a	n/a
web site optimization services	1 434	0.040	66 800 000	813	702	376	6 064	6 064	2.90	1.51
seo optimization	1 246	0.057	26 900 000	549 000	36 800	420	52 639	14	3.03	1.79
engine optimization	1 239	0.017	88 400 000	1 020 000	7 110	9	2 323	144 641	0.56	0.50
meta tag optimization	1 059	0.317	1 360 000	1 350	4	46	1 695	51 487	0.56	0.26
website optimization firm	964	0.030	1 310 000	445	813	198	40 717	1 171 696	1.00	0.61
search engine optimization training	919	0.044	44 200 000	520	230	236	7 854	222 714	2.00	1.50
web site optimization service	862	0.006	89 500 000	885	702	376	6 064	6 064	1.51	1.50
search engine optimization software										
optimization services										
meta optimization										
engine optimization search										
site optimization										
optimization software optimization s...										
search and engine and optimization										

4.9. Meta Tags and Other Places Waiting for your Keyword

META tags are HTML tags that provide information that describes the content of the webpages users will be viewing. META tags relate to the page as a whole and are not visible to human visitors in browsers. Initially these tags were meant to give the search engines information on what the page was about. By tweaking META tags and crowding them with any kind of keywords, relevant or irrelevant, it was easy to get your site ranking high for those terms. As time passed, search engines stopped considering META tags as a ranking factor at all, because they made them vulnerable to spammers.

This doesn't mean META tags do not require your attention. Some search engines use them to create a snippet for your page (it's a small description that appears below the link to your page in the search results). Having a great snippet means making people click on your page in the search results.

To optimize your META tags, make sure your keywords appear in the Description and Keywords tags.

If you open your page in the HTML source view, the META tags look something like this:

```
<meta name="keywords" content="keyword1, keyword2, keyword3" />
<meta name="description" content="keyword-rich description" />
```

Sometimes, the TITLE tag is also called a "META tag," but, strictly speaking, it isn't. Since the TITLE appears in the browser caption bar when someone is viewing your page, it is very important to have a relevant TITLE tag:

```
<TITLE>Keyword-rich and relevant title describing my page</TITLE>
```

TITLE is what search engines *do* take into consideration, and having a keyword-rich (not keyword-stuffed!) TITLE tag is great for your rankings.

Other places to put your keywords include:

Text links. By offering your visitors a link that says "more about personal computers" and "personal computers home page," you show them a way to find additional information about "personal computers." Search engines understand this, and your page receives more points for this keyphrase. It's good to have the page's keywords used in first three or four links on the page.

Headings. The tags "<h1>," "<h2>," "<h3>," "<h4>," "<h5>," "<h6>" create text headings of different importance on your page. Try to optimize at least the first one or two by placing your keyword in them. Search engines will understand that your keyword is important to the page if your headings contain it.

Bold tags. By embedding some words into the "<b>" or "<strong>" tag, you make it appear in bold. If your keywords are in bold somewhere on the page, it scores more for these words.

The first and the last paragraphs of the text. A search engine believes that you will use most important words at the beginning and at the end of your page's text.

Chapter 5

Mechanics of Organic Submission

5.1. Organic Growth

Search engines provide the opportunity to mark the path to your website. But in order to do this, you need to optimize your website for search engines. Linking and keyword optimization are only parts of search engine optimization. You also need to submit your website into search engines' indexes.

Before you get started, you should take a look at what each search engine accepts, the way it displays results, and the way it looks at a site's visible aspects like images and flash.

Make sure you know which landing page you want the users to go to. It does not necessarily need to be the home page, especially if you submit to a specialized search engine, in which case you want the landing page to be precisely related to the directory's subject. Otherwise, some searchers will think that you don't care enough to direct them to the right page, and will abandon the site after a few seconds.

It is the landing page that the directory or engine will link to, and therefore, it is the landing page that you want to submit. This mainly concerns submissions to directories.

Sometimes, however, you need to submit your home page. Most often it is the case with crawling search engines. The home page most often links to all sections of the website, or to the site map, so the search engine crawler will find all other pages of your website.

Most search engines accept listings free of charge. If your site is positioned properly, you don't really need paid inclusion since the best way to get your site submitted is still to have it linked from other websites.

Search engines post clear rules about how to submit your site. You can complete submission manually, but this takes a long time. Bear in mind that the number of submissions is not as important as the quality of the links.

5.2. Submission Software

"Submission Software" programs will automatically fill the submission forms of the search engines and directories, thus adding your site to hundreds of them while you just have to fill in your information once at the start.

The best submission software provides ways to verify submissions (i.e. after a certain time period after submission, check if the page has appeared in the SE results), and check the rankings of your submitted pages over a period of time.

Advanced submission software will also help you to submit internationally (e.g. into such important markets as Canada and Japan), offer not only web pages but also sitemaps, RSS feeds, alternative content (like audio, video and images) and products into special shopping engines such as Froogle.

Below are the most commonly used submission software packages:

Web CEO (www.webceo.com)
WebPosition Gold (www.webposition.com)
AddWeb (www.cyberspacehq.com)
IBP / Axandra (www.axandra.com)

Submission process can be either automated or manual. Some engines protect themselves from automatic submission, but about 90% do allow it. Therefore, it's a good idea to use submission software, which will make your life a lot easier because besides the actual submission, the software usually offers useful features like site analysis and rank check.

Some programs (e.g. Web CEO) combine automatic and manual submission. They will also try to facilitate even the manual ones for you by pre-filling forms, so the only thing left for you is to fill in the special graphic code used for protection against auto-submission (the software cannot recognize it).

Figure 5.1. Top Submission Software Programs

	Web CEO webceo.com	**WebPosition Gold** **webposition.com**	AddWeb cyberspacehq. com	**IBP (Axandra)** **axandra.com**
General	**Unlimited use**	**30-day trial**	**30-day trial**	**30-day trial, during which you aren't able to submit**
Tool name	Submission Tool	Submitter	Submission	SE Submitter
Automated submission to search engines	170+	138	197	150
Guided manual submission to search engines	Yes (30 engines) + ability to include in reports	Yes (5 engines) + ability to include in reports	Yes (11 Engines)	Yes (200+ engines)
Auto verification of compliance with SE rules	Yes	Yes	Yes	Yes
Manual submission emulation	Yes	Yes	Yes	Yes
Automatic repopulation of keywords and descriptions from META tags	Yes	No	No	No
Group changing of submission rules	Yes	No	No	No
Scanning site for pages available for submission	Yes	Yes	No	No
Viewing real SE responses	Yes	Yes	Yes	No

Figure 5.2. Submission List in Web CEO

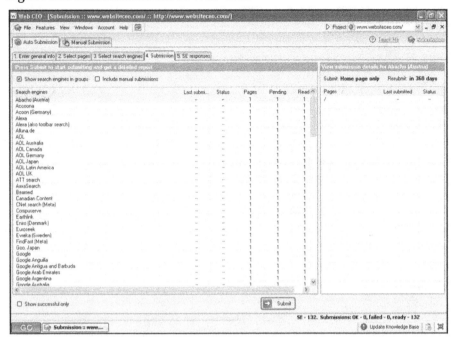

Let's use the example of Web CEO to demonstrate the flow of the submission process. We chose it because you can use its submission tool without limitations, even in the free edition.

Web CEO is very easy to use. It takes you through all the necessary steps with its functional interface. One of the above screenshots illustrates the Web CEO's submission tool. Here you start submitting your site, check progress, and most importantly, see the results in real-time.

Web CEO can automatically retrieve your site description and keywords from your META tags before each submission, and complies with the rules of each search engine that is in its database. That is, it will submit your home page only and resubmit not earlier than a year later, if recommended by a given search engine (you can change these settings manually).

Figure 5.3. Submission List in AddWeb

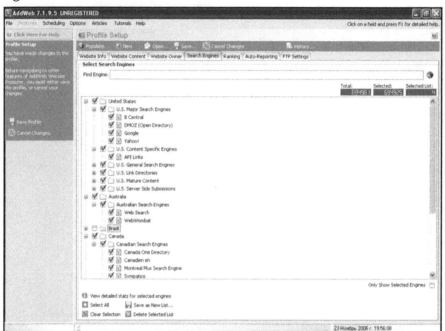

Pay attention after you complete submission through the software; you need to *verify* if your site is actually submitted and how it is listed. Web CEO allows immediate submission verification through viewing real search engines' responses, and indexation verification through the special ranking 'indexed pages' report (you'll have to switch to another tool, "ranking checker").

Generally, you do not need to resubmit your site to any search engine, although many marketing sources would tell you otherwise. The fact is if you do it right the first time, you should not have to resubmit. However, if you do want to resubmit your website, make sure you familiarize yourself with each search engines' regulations on how often you can submit. They usually allow submission every few weeks. You need to comply with the rules, and avoid submitting too often.

Many search engines accept listings through partnerships, so it is often cheaper to get listed through those partnerships (called "backdoors") instead of direct paid inclusion.

Figure 5.4. Submission List in IBP (Axandra's Software)

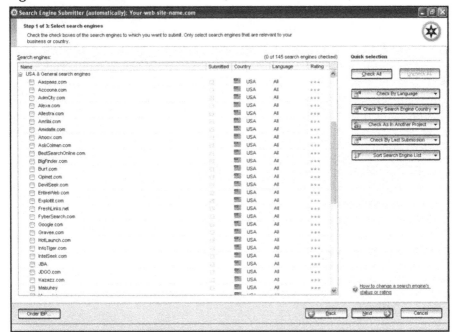

5.3. Submission Myths

There are a number of false statements that sometimes can be heard about the submission process. Although these statements are more and more seldom as many people become more optimization-savvy. Don't let yourself be fooled by marketing and optimization companies that try to sell on you using them.

"Submit to as many engines as you can." Most traffic to your site is driven by a couple of major search engines (namely, Google, Yahoo!, and MSN). The remaining 10% of traffic will come from a number of smaller engines put together (but not more that a hundred or so). Submission to thousands of search engines is a waste of time and it will never help your rankings. Submission is nothing but placing your page in a queue of pages that await indexation. Submission software aims at facilitating the process and the control of results — that's all. This myth was invented by optimization companies that were eager to make their service lists longer and change even more for the same service and results.

However, the capability of submitting to directories is a good bonus to any SEO software. Just remember that most directories require manual submission. If the software claims to "automatically submit your site to 60,000 directories," its place is in your recycling bin. Most of those directories are link farms and suspicious link directories all banned by the search engines long ago.

Another well-known myth is that a website, once submitted, needs constant and frequent resubmission in order to maintain rankings.

Today major search engines, having found your website, will crawl it and update the copy in their database regularly anyway, whether you will resubmit or not. The more frequently your site is updated with fresh content, the more often the search spider comes to get updated on the news. Resubmission may make sense once a year, only if the crawler hasn't really dropped in for quite a while.

GoogleBot (Google's robot that reads pages and stores it in Google's index) will visit your site within four weeks after submission, and so will the other engines. Google updates its database on a monthly basis. Once your pages are listed, they are constantly revised and updated.

5.4. Submission to Individual Search Engines

This section outlines the specifics of submission into each major search engine.

Google submission

Website: www.google.com
Free submission URL: http://www.google.com/addurl.html

With its powerful robot, Google constantly adds new sites to its index and re-indexes the existing ones. To speed up the process of adding your site, Google offers a page where you can choose "add URL," entering your page in the queue of pages awaiting indexation. However, Google does not guarantee that adding the URL in this manner will inevitably result in adding the page into the index.

In the form where you add your URL, you need to specify the address of your page (including the http:// prefix), and also add some comments that describe the site contents.

Google recommends that only the home page be submitted, and claims its robot will find the rest of pages by following links. We recommend that you add several of your most prominent pages, because the robot's behavior once on the site is unpredictable: it can index a hundred pages at once or visit a hundred times, indexing one page at a time.

As a rule, you want to submit your home page, your site map, your site sections or categories' home pages, plus the pages recently updated.

Paid Submission URL: adwords.google.com

Paid submission in Google is in fact its PPC (pay-per-click) advertising system, AdWords. You place your ad bidding for certain keywords, Google shows your ad when someone searches for these keywords and charges you if its visitor clicks on your ad (and thus comes to your site from Google).

AdWords ads are shown in the special "sponsored links" column next to the organic results, and may also be distributed in the AdSense context advertising network (affiliate websites that show relevant AdWords ads on their pages).

Google has a powerful click-fraud protection mechanism and allows for configuring many paid campaigns options that will be discussed later in the book. You can set up a "training" account to play around before setting up a serious ad campaign.

Yahoo! Submission

Website: www.yahoo.com
Free submission URL: http://search.yahoo.com/info/submit.html

Yahoo!'s free submission service is integrated with its "Site Explorer" feature that analyzes your site by showing backlinks and indexed pages. To add your site, type the URL (including the http:// prefix). The search engine's robot will re-index your site by following links from the pages you entered in this manner.

Besides submitting web pages, Yahoo! offers a possibility to submit a "site feed". You can add your RSS Feed (supported formats are RSS 0.9, RSS 1.0, RSS 2.0, Atom 0.3) or simply enter a path to a text file that contains a list of URLs of pages that are on your site. Yahoo! will crawl them all.

Other types of content accepted through free submission are "mobile site" (xHTML, WML, cHTML format), and "media RSS" – a new type of RSS feed in the RSS 2.0 format that handles various media types, such as short films or TV, in addition to providing additional metadata with the media. Media RSS enables content publishers and bloggers to broadly distribute descriptions of and links to multimedia content.

Paid submission

Yahoo! paid submission is called Yahoo! Search Submit, featuring such services as:
Sponsored Search is a pay-per-click pricing model similar to Microsoft AdCenter and Google AdWords. It takes a minimum $5 deposit to open

a Sponsored Search account and your click-through charges (the cost you pay per click) are deducted from this amount. However, Yahoo! recommends that your initial deposit equals your projected monthly budget. You can spend as much or as little as you like each month based on the keywords you select and how much you bid for each one.

Product Submit – submit your products to Yahoo! Shopping[15], and they will appear in highly relevant areas across Yahoo!, giving you access to millions of motivated buyers. Inclusion in Yahoo! Product Search[16] and buyer's guide pages[17] is based on a cost-per-click price that varies by product category. You pay only for leads directly to your site.

Travel Submit – detailed listings of your travel offers and deals will be featured in relevant areas across Yahoo! Travel[18]. You pay only for leads directed to your site. Inclusion is based on cost-per-click (CPC) pricing that varies by travel listing category.

Directory Submit – Yahoo! Directory Submit is part of a suite of services created to help businesses like yours get more out of Yahoo!, more efficiently. Whether you've submitted to the Yahoo! Directory in the past or are a new user, Yahoo! Directory Submit provides an expedited review of web sites you propose for the Yahoo! Directory.

Regional Categories

If your site targets or discusses a specific regional market, you need to submit to a regional category. For example, if your site is about a flower shop in Paris, France, you would need to submit it to the regional Yahoo! category:

Directory > Regional > Countries > France > Regions > Ile-de-France > Departments > Paris > Business and Shopping > Shopping and Services > **Flowers**

. . . and not the general Yahoo! flower category:

Directory > Business and Economy > Shopping and Services > **Flowers**

---

[15] http://shopping.yahoo.com
[16] http://search.yahoo.com/products
[17] http://help.yahoo.com/l/us/yahoo/ysm/ps/basics/basics-06.html
[18] http://travel.yahoo.com

Variations of Descriptions

It is useful to submit a slightly different description of your site for each initial directory submission – that way you can estimate which descriptions are the most compelling to attract people to visit your website and also which directories are providing the most traffic to your website.

Many directories feed their database results to search engines and directories, so if you have a description unique to each directory and you see that description pop up on other search sites, you know it is the result of that original directory submission and immediately recognize the value of that original submission.

Remember that directory editors don't care about your site's ranking in their search results. If they are reviewing a site submission that contains an obviously keyword stuffed title and description, they are unlikely to find it appealing or beneficial for inclusion in their database.

Always make sure your submission details are relevant, interesting, and most importantly, accurate. Try to highlight your site's benefits for the visitor and unique content that makes it stand out from others in the same category. If your site sounds just like a cookie-cutter version of others in your topic there is no incentive for the editor to include it or for surfers to visit it.

Submitting to the Yahoo! Directory

Submission into Yahoo! Directory is critical because it is so popular around the world. You can get listed quickly trough Yahoo!'s paid Express Submission service for $299. However, even with this service, your site's inclusion in the directory, site placement or site commentary is not guaranteed. One of the Yahoo! employees will review your site and consider your suggestions within seven business days.

You do not have to pay to be included, but you need to be extra cautious and thorough because the way you submit your site will influence your site's ranking in the directory. You need to do research before you submit and pay special attention when choosing the most appropriate category. You also need to be extremely careful when writing your description, making sure it contains your main keywords without being too wordy. If you are not confident about your category and description, you can contract a marketing firm to handle the submission for you. If you are not sure, it really makes sense to go to professionals because having the right category and description will pay off in the long term.

Here's an example of a successful site description for Yahoo!:

ABC VIP Adventures – offers tailored adventure travel and vacation packages to New Zealand including day tours, exotic corporate trips, luxury travel packages, kite surfing, and extreme sports.

Example of an unsuccessful site description for Yahoo!:

ABC Travel – we are the best! We are the only company to contact for your vacation. Call now!

The latter does not use the actual company name, plus it contains lots of hype but lacks keywords and clues as to what the site is about. In this case, the Yahoo! editor would have to visit the site submitted and come up with their own description, and it's doubtful the edited description will be something the submitter would be happy with.

Submitting to Open Directory

Submission into Open Directory is crucial because DMOZ is used by a large number of portals and sites, so once a site is included in DMOZ it can be found in other directories like Pandia Plus and Google Directory.

http://www.dmoz.org/add.html

DMOZ is run entirely by volunteers and is extremely understaffed. Your site submission must be hand-reviewed by one of the volunteers before it can be considered for inclusion. Therefore, it can take six months or more before your submission is reviewed, so you must be patient. You should submit your site, then wait three months and follow up with an email to the category editor; then wait three months and write an email to the category editor above your category; then wait three months and ask for help in the Open Directory Public Forum[19]; then wait one month and write to DMOZ senior staff & post to various forums seeking help if you still have not seen your listing. Just be patient and persistent.

---

[19] **http://www.resource-zone.com**

Rules of Submission

Do it once: Despite the hype, there is NEVER a need to resubmit to a search engine or directory unless your site is dropped entirely (which is very rare).

Do it properly: Be very thorough when submitting, especially to directories. Take the time to research and locate the most appropriate category for your site.

Be brief: Don't waffle on about your site in the description field. Get to the point and describe your site in a short sentence or two.

Be accurate: Don't try to trick potential visitors by using vague or misleading descriptions about your products or services.

Be relevant: There is a fine line to tread between relevance and keyword optimization when creating your site descriptions for submissions. Try not to cross it by using descriptions over-stuffed with keywords.

Be humble: "Best Web Site in the World!!" is not going to convince anyone and may earn you the wrath of search engine editors.

Be patient: Search engines and directories can take up to six months to index and list your site. Re-submitting won't help things and could result in your site being shoved to the bottom of the review pile.

The directory submission process can be time-consuming, but taking a little bit of time and care with your submissions can pay dividends for your site for years.

You can use also paid directory submission provided by the sites listed below:

Figure 5.5. Top Paid Directories

http://dir.yahoo.com $299
http://directory.v7n.com $50
http://www.01webdirectory.com $49
http://www.sunsteam.com $45
http://www.goguides.org $70
http://www.allestra.com $39
http://www.botw.org $100 annually or $249 one-time
http://www.123world.com $199 annually
http://www.arielis.com $30
http://www.incrawler.com $25
http://www.uncoverthenet.com $59 annually or $159 one-time
http://www.cannylink.com $20
http://www.rlrouse.com $50
http://www.thisisouryear.com $25
http://www.allwebdirectory.com $29
http://www.1st-spot.net $15
http://www.linkopedia.com $10
http://www.aroundtheweb.com $15
http://www.searchturtle.com $20
http://www.informationoutpost.com $5
http://www.ajdee.com $25
http://www.skaffe.com Free/$45
http://www.web-beacon.com Free/$40
http://www.joeant.com Free/$40
http://www.gimpsy.com $49
http://www.wowdirectory.com Free/$43

Chapter 6

Making Friends in the Jungle

6.1. Linking

Linking is one of the determining factors of your website's ranking. Search engine spiders evaluate the number and the quality of links on your website by looking at the text in the links and to where they lead. Links are the number one ranking criteria in all major search engines. Links allow you to embed yourself into the Jungle naturally, and strengthen and develop your Jungle family.

Links allow your website to grow organically and provide a means for long-term survival.

Links can be inbound (another website links to yours), outbound (you link to another site) and reciprocal (you both link to each other). You do not need to reciprocate every link; if the information on your site is relevant and useful, those who you connect with should understand the benefits of linking to you. You simply need to explain how your link will benefit the host website.

When you are just starting out, you might be inclined to get any links possible onto your website to build up your rank. But remember that in the Jungle people judge you by who you link with, so avoid linking to porn, gambling, drug and terrorism sites because they will ruin your reputation. It is always better to link to credible sites because you will get a much higher ranking and save face.

Since the world's leading search engine, Google, uses the authority of inbound links to rank your website, it virtually forces you to engage in active link development. So the first question you ask is: "OK, how do I get quality links?" You *could* sit and wait until someone discovers your site and says, "Wow, it's a great one, let's link to it." However your own initiative will be far more rewarding.

Link partners are found with the help of the same thing you use to find anything else on the Internet – the search engines.

You enter your keywords into the search engine, and get the list of relevant resources. Some of them will be your competitors, and all the others are potential link partners!

You shouldn't hope that every contact will result in a linking deal. Some will bounce or not respond, some will ask that you link back or pay for the link. Whether you agree or not depends on your budget and how seriously you take search engine marketing. Here are the golden rules to keep in mind when you consider purchasing or exchanging a link:

The link must be from a relevant website. It may be a vertical/industry-specific directory, an encyclopedia or a catalog; an educational website covering your topic – whatever, the linking page should contain your keywords or at least be relevant for them.

The link text should contain your keywords where possible. Insist that your link exchange partners put keywords in the link text, or supply them the ready HTML code of the link.

It is desirable, though not obligatory, that the link comes from a website with a high page rank, so it maximally contributes to your own. Nonetheless, there's nothing bad about exchanging links with a rank lower than yours, provided the sites are relevant.

When you have exchanged a link, check the linking page for the source code. If the link contains a "rel=nofollow" attribute, this link will only refer you traffic but will not contribute to your page rank.

There's an alternative way of finding link partners. Find out who links to your competitors. If those resources are independent (i.e., not affiliated with your competitors), they could link to you as well!

This kind of research is done by typing "*link:www.example.com*" (using the name of your competitor's site, of course) in search engines (we recommend using all three big guns for this, to get the longest list). Thus, you will see all sites that link to *www.example.com.*

Why is linking so important?

Ask search engine experts how rankings depend on quantity and quality of inbound links. Answers will all be different: "significantly depends," "considerably depends," "critically depends" and the like – you get the point. No links, no rankings.

A search engine's logic needs no explanation. You can consider your site pretty important, but if others do not, they won't link to you. If no one except yourself thinks you're notable, why put your site up in the search results? And vice versa: if your site is full of relevant information worth referring to, and is constantly updated so it is not easy to duplicate, people will understand the value you bring into the Jungle. The search engines, knowing that you are respected by the community, will take you high in their ranks.

Every link given to your by another website is a vote cast for you by that site in the process of top ten election.

Quality and quantity of inbound links are considered by Google when calculating PageRank™. PageRank[20] is a figure that measures importance of each Web page Google knows about. This importance doesn't depend on which keywords you use – it's absolute. However, many SEO experts believe PageRank matters when Google hands out tickets for the first ten seats.

In this manner, Google proves the main law of the Jungle: You can pretend to be the king, demonstrating your strong muscles of textual content or bright feathers of visual design, but if others don't cast a vote (link) for you, the wise search engines won't crown you as such.

Link Sources

Depending on how we acquire them, we divide the links into four kinds:

One-way inbound links. This kind of link doesn't oblige you to put a link back from your page to the linking site. Such links appear naturally if other webmasters sincerely value your content and consider it worth referring their visitors to. Search engines love these links most, because they are most difficult to acquire.

---

[20]   http://www.google.com/technology

Reciprocal (two-way) links. You ask a potential partner to link to you, and tell them you will place (or have already placed) a link back from your page. These links are valued by the search engines less than one-way links: they might testify not only mutual respect for each other between you and your link partner, but also a common interest in boosting rankings. However, don't be afraid to exchange links with a relevant website – this makes your linking policy look natural. Any website that grows naturally always has both kinds of links.

Paid links. Many websites do not officially sell links, but it is possible to negotiate and buy a link from them – if you are not worst competitors and enemies, of course. Besides, there are numerous "link brokers" that will search and buy link opportunities for your money. An example of such a service is **www.textlinkbrokers.com**. When you purchase links, remember that search engines strongly discourage this kind of promotion. The websites that are selling links explicitly are often blacklisted by the search engines (or will be blacklisted in the near future). Also, link brokers do not always tell you the real price for a link. Google PR and Alexa traffic ranks are not the best criteria to estimate what a link partnership might give you. Always look at the relevancy first, and on the power (PR and ATR) second. If you believe a link isn't worth what your link broker tells you, don't hesitate to negotiate a lower price that better fits into your budget.

Directory and content resource links. As a rule, directories such as DMOZ and JoeAnt.com are edited manually, and if you ask to add your site, the decision is made by a human – the person responsible for the appropriate category. Some directories are free, and others will require that you pay for getting into the index.

In any case, directory pages usually have high PageRanks and they are indexed by the search engines in the first turn. If you are registered under a relevant category, it's a considerable bonus for your rankings.

In order to get links from directories, you need to submit your website, usually by filling out an online form. Some directories will only list your site's name, but many include a description. Directory listings are reviewed by people, so make their lives easier by submitting all the necessary information. This way, you ensure that your listing appears quickly and in the way you want. Read the submission tips and see how other sites in your category are listed, but use original copy to state what sets you apart from competition.

You can look up industry-specific directories by searching for "your keyword + directory" or "keyword + submit site" or "your keyword + add URL."

Content resources (such as article sites) will link back to you after you submit certain content (an article, news item or review) to them. They do not guarantee that the page that holds your article will receive high PageRank or traffic. However, such resources are often indexed by search engines, so it's a nice way to get a quality and relevant inbound link.

Links could be from a number of sources, and it is always better to attach relevant text to the links on your site because search engines look at the text as part of their ranking evaluation. The best way to build links is to include your keywords as well as a description of the site you link with. This way, you increase the keyword density of your website and rank higher. However, search engines penalize those who repeat the same keywords in links because it is a sure indication of manipulating search engines to rank your website higher. There are no set rules on this. Therefore, mix up the text in your links to appear as natural as possible.

Linking is the best way to make your network grow and improve your ranking in the long term. Besides expanding your site organically, linking delivers specialized quality traffic to your site, which translates into higher conversions and click-through rates.

Link Exchange

After selecting your potential link partners, start corresponding with them. If you are not sure whether the response will be positive, take the first move and place a backlink on your site before writing a link exchange request. Giving a short, concise and positive review of the resource you are requesting to link with is considered a good courtesy. So write some constructive ideas, mention that your site is relevant to theirs, and you've already placed a link from your page, and then ask to link back.

If your link exchange request is ignored or declined, try following up with a letter offering to purchase a link.

It is always a good idea to explore the website you are going to exchange links with before writing. After all, it may end up being your competitor!

Affiliate Program Links

Most affiliate programs redirect your links through their websites, and some add query strings to the links for tracking purposes. Therefore, you will not gain in page rank or link popularity by adding these links. We do, however, recommend affiliate links because they build up your brand, and create awareness and trust in the eyes of potential customers.

If you have a good business and can afford paying commission, you can create an affiliate network for quick distribution around the Internet – it is like sowing grass, some seeds will grow and some will die out. Of course, having an affiliate network requires substantial effort. You need to feed the network with products, news and customer support. You also have to realize that some of the merchants are going to fail, but some will become powerful sellers.

There are also large affiliate networks you can join if you do not want to set up a network of your own, for example: **www.linkconnector.com** and **www.commissionjunction.com**. Good affiliate networks offer tracking and commission management tools as well as help drive traffic to your website. You might want to try out one of the programs to see whether setting up a network of your own is feasible.

Link Management Tools

Figuring out who will be your next link partner can become a tiresome task. Several software packages were invented to help with the job. We will illustrate their use with the help of Web CEO Link Analysis and Partner Finder tools.

Web CEO is a single software package for site promotion, analysis and maintenance which can be downloaded from **www.webceo.com** (you can also find the package on the CD that comes with this book).

When you open Web CEO and choose "Analyze Link Popularity," you will see five reports that you can run, among them "My Site." Add your competitor as a site and see how many inbound links they've got. You will get an estimate of what you need to achieve to outrun them. We recommend using Yahoo! or MSN for this analysis, because Google has a notorious habit of concealing the most relevant links used to make up rankings.

The most valuable report is "who links to me," which allows you to add your competitor as a researched site and see who exactly links to them, thus contributing to their rankings. Here you get a list that you will then mail to requesting link exchange.

The "Link Text Analysis" helps you determine what keywords are used in links that point to a website, yours or your competitor's. Keywords used in inbound links are those your website will get high rankings for.

Finally you can use the "Linking Sites Overview" report to find out who's linking to more than one of your competitors (i.e. those sites that are independent or not affiliated with your competitors). If a website links to several leaders, there's a high chance that if it links to you this will help you become a leader, too.

Running the scan again several days after the first one will help you build the history of link popularity changes and see the picture in dynamics, thus keeping up with what's going on in the Jungle. It becomes even easier because Web CEO includes a task scheduler which will run tasks for you automatically.

Figure 6.1. Link Analysis Tool in Web CEO

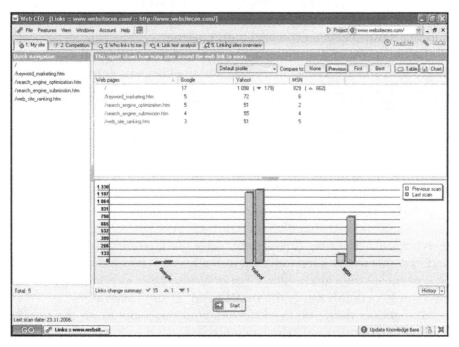

Now let's see whether it is possible to automate another process: the correspondence with the potential link partners. As soon as you have compiled the list of websites you'd like to get links from, you need to somehow contact them and not to lose track of your correspondence with each.

Web CEO has a tool for that purpose called "Partner Finder." The underlying process illustrates the fast and effective link management strategy.

By entering your potential link sites on the "Search for Partners" tab, you get their "SE score" that shows you how important those sites are considered by the search engines and how relevant they are (by analyzing their META and TITLE tags) to your theme.

You can send bulk as well as personalized messages from within this program. We recommend personalized correspondence with the websites that are especially important for your rankings, and using the bulk feature for the rest. The program includes several templates for link exchange request letters so you have something to start with.

Email addresses of webmasters are then extracted automatically from their websites, from WHOIS information and Alexa site business card. At least the software does its best to do this, but from our experience you have to oversee the process and help manually where necessary.

Now that you have all necessary knowledge and tools, and are warned about the dangers on the long but rewarding path of website promotion, nothing stands between you and high rankings.

Some words are left to say about the tools that help you watch your progress as you go. These are called ranking check tools or programs.

6.2. Ranking

After optimizing pages, submitting them to search engines and acquiring links, you are ready for the ranking check.

This process shows what results have been achieved. Much effort and time was put into selecting keywords, tweaking pages, developing link popularity. This labor must bring fruit: top rankings.

There's evidence that Web surfers rarely get down to page five or six of search results. As a rule, three result pages (30 top results) are enough to find what one needs. Each website is only allowed to occupy one (maximum two) positions for a given query; if one website is not so relevant, then the next would certainly satisfy the user's need for information.

To become visible on the Internet, your page should hit the top 30. Ideally, it is found among the top ten results.

If your site has got into an index, but its position is not as auspicious as you expected, don't panic. You need to analyze the work done, correct the flaws, study current leaders and try again. Leaders' rankings are subject to constant change, and in order to survive in this race, you need to raise your head above the competition, to watch it and frequently upgrade.

Keeping the ranking history of your site also has its strong points. Regular ranking fluctuations that result from search engines' updates will tell you when to expect a decrease in organic traffic flow and compensate with extensive pay-per-click campaigns. If your rankings have shifted down one or several points, and don't get restored for a long time, most likely you've been displaced by a stronger competitor.

Watching your positions on a number of search engines for numerous keywords, comparing yourself to competitors and to your own positions a month ago, tracking the history, etc., can be easy – again, only if you have the right tools.

Several web promotion packages have offered such tools, among them IBP, Web CEO and WebPosition.

Advanced ranking check tools like that of Web CEO also offer additional possibilities, for instance, finding out which pages of yours and competitors' websites are in the indexes of which search engines, or calculating a "balance score," a single figure that summarizes your or your competitor's overall visibility in a given moment. In Web CEO, this report is called "ranking score".

The balance or ranking score is calculated using a formula, which includes the weight of each search engine (for instance, positions on Google may matter more than Baidu) and for each position in the top ten list. It also considers the number of pages a search engine finds from your website.

Having this figure for your site and comparing it to your competitor, you can determine how prominent you've become in the Jungle. More important, you can compare the number of points you've scored today and to those from a month ago, to see whether your overall visibility has increwased through constant ranking fluctuations and whether you're on the right path.

Attitudes toward Ranking Tools and Search Engines

Ranking tools are convenient because they offer great speed and productivity. They can handle large amounts of data and present it in neat and easy-to-understand reports.

The problem with the ranking checkers is that search engines discourage automatic queries. They can ban your computer (not website, thank goodness!) from sending any more queries in a given day if they detect numerous and frequent requests issued by ranking checkers.

Figure 6.2. Web CEO Ranking Check Tool

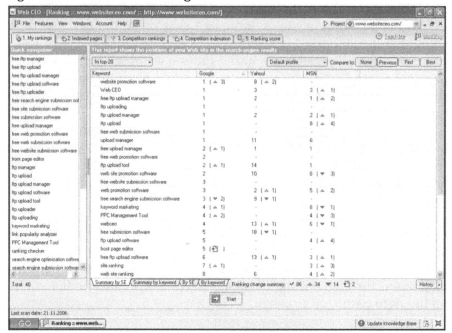

As a solution, advanced ranking checkers offer human emulation options. IBP uses browser emulation and manipulates cookies. Web CEO imitates a human surfer that works through a web browser by taking random pauses between search requests, using proxy servers, masquerading as different user-agents (browsers), visiting search engines' home pages before passing the query, and downloading images and styles bound to the pages.

Builing ranking history in Web CEO is done in a way similar to link popularity history. Web CEO automatically saves the results of each scan, so you only have to schedule scans to run regularly with the help of an onboard scheduler. In a several weeks, you will be able to proudly look at the neat ranking charts generated by the program. You can track your and your competitor's ranking history as well as indexation history.

Finally, remember that rankings, although an important progress indicator, are not the final diagnosis for your site. The increasing amount of traffic, high conversion and return rates, satisfied customers' testimonials, and your bank account balance – there are so many ways to measure success! A ranking tool is only a means to understand whether you cope with the primary task – becoming visible and prominent in the Internet Jungle.

Chapter 7

Setting Traps

If you want to jump-start your website and you are willing to pay for it, there are some shortcuts. However, simply paying for your advertisements does not solve all problems.

The fact is, with paid ads you need to have a strategy and understanding of how search marketing works in order to reap the full benefits. Therefore, many times it makes sense to seek the help of professionals to manage paid advertisements. This is especially true for those industries that are extremely competitive in the online market. Aggressive companies contract SEO specialists to monitor their bidding on keywords and use techniques and tricks to get the rest to overspend their marketing dollars and eventually exit the market.

7.1. Paid and Sponsored Advertisements

In the Internet Jungle, it takes time and effort to build your popularity. While you are waiting for your organic ranking to kick in, you can pay search engines and directories to stream traffic to your site by displaying your listing at the top of the search results.

This strategy takes a number of forms, but in any case the premise is the same: you pay for your food (clicks) according to the pricing structure you choose. You can pay per click, per lead or per phone call.

PPC stands for pay-per-click. This system and the like are popular because they give immediate results, and, more importantly, provide a highly tractable marketing medium. You can see the correlation between your ad dollar spent and the difference in sales numbers. However, sometimes sales is not the immediate goal (a company may just want to build brand recognition), so the correlation might not be as important.

Pay-Per-Click

PPC originated in 1998 when Overture offered contextual-based advertising for sale. The system offered by Overture sprouted into a highly competitive marketing medium.

PPC has many applications, and is especially useful for testing ideas and market conditions. By testing new business models and products with PPC, you can estimate whether your new idea is going to be successful before you invest in it.

PPC allows you to see if the market is ready for your new idea, and whether you are marketing your idea the right way, to the right audience.

Larger PPC engines are popular because they offer better quality traffic, support tools, and the ease of managing multiple accounts. Smaller search engines are more susceptible to fraud and some never have real traffic, so choose your search engines wisely.

Yahoo! Search Marketing (formerly Overture)

In late 2003, Overture became a wholly-owned subsidiary of Yahoo! Inc., and in spring 2005 it was renamed Yahoo! Search Marketing. Overture is used for pay-per-click in the Yahoo! search results. Yahoo! Search Advertising network includes AltaVista, AllTheWeb and DogPile search engines, so your ads may also show up on those engines. Some time ago Overture fed paid listings to MSN, but now Microsoft Live Search has its own advertising solution called AdCenter.

Figure 7.1. Yahoo! Overture PPC

Google AdWords

Google AdWords (**www.google.com/adwords**) (Figure 7.2.) currently is one of the most effective Pay-Per-Click management systems. It is also very expensive, so you need to watch your ROI on daily or hourly bases.

Figure 7.2. Google Adwords PPC

With Google AdWords you can create your own customized target area by designating a geographical radius or boundary and, should you need to adverise internationally, Google AdWords offers the option to target your ads in 38 different languages, throughout hundreds of countries. There's no minimum spending requirement (against that of $5 at YSM), cost-per-click could be as low as one cent.

You can choose to display your ads in Google results only, or spread them over Google's search partners network (that includes such engines as AOL, Netscape, Earthlink, Lycos, Ask.com, and Dogpile), or even show them on the websites that belong to Google's context advertising network (AdSense). Any webmaster can subscribe to AdSense and add AdWords ads (including yours) to their site.

Live Search (MSN) AdCenter

Live Search Advertising (**https://adcenter.microsoft.com**) was presented by Microsoft at SES 2006 Conference in NY. The new Microsoft AdCenter has already increased the number of searches by approximatly 70% of traffic.

Figure 7.3. MSN Search Advertising

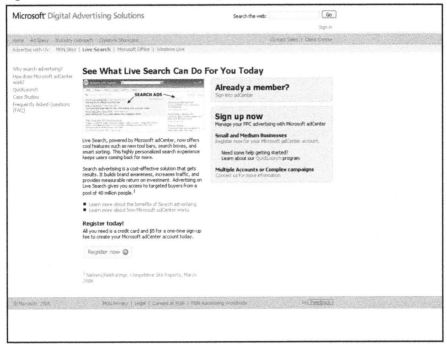

Live Search generates one of the best conversion rates across major search engines. AdCenter allows you to track your keyword performance, helping you target your desired market segments and execute intelligent bid decisions. Live Search PPC engine offers rich demographic data and a keyword tool, and gives the flexibility and control to make rapid adjustments to the client's website.

Ask Sponsored Listing

Ask Sponsored Listings (**http://sponsoredlistings.ask.com**) are an automated pay-per-click solution that offers results on Ask and Ask syndication networks, including Mamma, Mysearch, CNET.com, Infospace, Dogpile, Excite and others.

Pay-Per-Lead

PPL is an online advertising payment model, in which payment is based solely on qualifying leads. In a pay-per-lead agreement, advertisers *only* pay for leads generated at their destination site. You do not pay for visitors who don't sign up.

A lead is generally a sign-up form involving contact information and perhaps some demographic information; it is typically a non-cash conversion event. A lead may consist of as little as an email address, or it may involve a detailed form covering multiple pages.

One risk PPL advertisers have is the potential of fraudulent activities. Some marketing firms offering PPL campaigns offer incentive programs to third parties or marketing partners to register and fill out lead forms. Some false leads are easy to spot. Nonetheless, it is advisable to make a regular audit of the results. Be sure to choose a reputable company as your PPL provider.

Here are some of the more popular PPL programs:

Fastclick jumped on the scene about a year ago and has quickly become a webmaster favorite. They specialize in both CPC banner ads and very lucrative pop-unders. Many webmasters swear by this program as the one that really "pays the bills."

Commission Junction has grown to be one of many top performers for webmasters. They offer literally thousands of offers from hundreds of merchants, with a good variety of both affiliate and pay-per-lead programs, including top brands like eBay, Overture, CompUSA, Yahoo! and MSN.

Casale Media is a newcomer, but has quickly caught the eye of many webmasters as a top-notch CPM and pop-under network. The Casale Media program is highly recommended for all webmasters to check out.

Direct Leads offers a wide variety of pay-per-lead, pay-per-click and co-registration offers. They have a strong reputation in the industry and webmasters highly recommend them. Like all programs here, this is a top earner for many.

Pay-Per-Acquisition (or Pay-Per-Action)

PPA is an online advertising payment model in which the advertiser *only* pays for the leads that finish in a sale for the customer. Usually, the advertiser receives a percentage of the sale amount. This model is popular because it is straightforward in terms of numbers, and often advertisers take on the set-up cost, so you do not have to pay anything until you actually make a sale originated from one of the advertiser's leads[21].

Pay-Per-Call

Recently, advertisers introduced an option where you pay for every call you receive to a designated 1-800 number given to you by the pay-per-call company. In the pay-per-call model, sponsored ads display a toll-free phone number and a link to a brief information page about the business instead of a link to your website.

Figure 7.4. AOL Pay-Per-Call

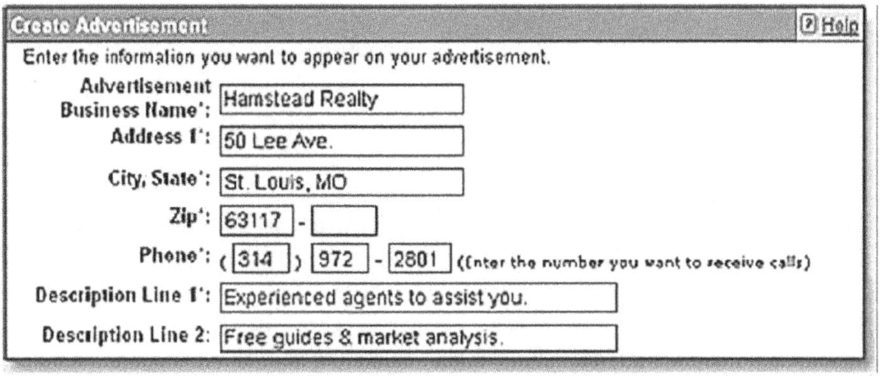

The pay-per-call format solves a problem for the millions of businesses that don't have a web presence, but still want to be found by online surfers. It's especially effective for local businesses, since pay-per-call ads can be targeted for users in a specific location.

Pay-per-call is also appealing to any business that performs best with a high-touch presence. When people are motivated enough to pick up the

---

[21] At SES2006 REVShare **www.revsharetv.com** – television's largest broker of performance based advertisement – presented a lead generation program. REVShare offers complete support for WEB, SMS Text Messaging, 800 and Interactive Technolgies. One is differences between REVShare's Model and the traditional model of CPA Televison is that the REVShare network distribution system eliminates 95% of costs and allows for expedited delivery to over 700 Stations, when CPA Televison distribution of commercial is difficult, time consuming and expensive.

phone and call, they are often closer to making a purchase than people who simply click through on a sponsored online listing. Phone reps can answer questions and overcome objections more quickly than most websites can.

AOL is spotlighting pay-per-call ads in search results, giving them top billing over paid search listings, citing that they want to make sure they give advertisers that jump into this program presence.

But pay-per-call ads are generally more expensive than pay-per-click advertisements. Advertisers need to decide for themselves whether the return on investment warrants the greater expense of the program.

At this point, AOL displays just a single pay-per-call ad on each search result page, but this may change in the future if the program proves successful. AOL will also display both pay-per-call and sponsored links from the same advertisers under some conditions; no effort is currently being made to avoid duplication. This provides a unique opportunity for search marketers to gain up to three positions on a search result page – through algorithmic results, paid links or pay-per-call listings.

Google provides both algorithmic and paid search results to AOL Search. The new pay-per-call listings are provided by Ingenio: **www.ingenio. com**. Ingenio serves pay-per-call ads in the same way that Google provides sponsored links to AOL. And like Google, Ingenio distributes pay-per-call listings to multiple properties beyond AOL[22].

This distribution deal gives exposure to pay-per-call ads on properties such as Excite, NBCi, Search.com and MetaCrawler, and Yellow Pages directory SuperPages.com powered by Pay For Calls (PFC) by Verizon[23].

---

[22] At AOL Search, the following information about your business will appear in the Sponsored Links section:
"Your business name"
"Your business description, address, city, state"
"The phone icon, Call Locally, Toll Free: 800-555-5555"
With Ingenio Pay-Per-Call, the businesses can acquire new customers online – and pay only after they receive an incoming phone call.

[23] With SuperPages.com you have two types of performance based ads to choose from: Pay-Per-Click and Pay For Calls, similar to Pay-Per-Call at Ingenio. You can track and manage the performance results at **my.superpages. com/manage** or by calling 1-800-428-8722.

At SES 2006, NY, Who's Calling **www.whoscalling.com** has presented a set of tracking phone numbers which can be offered as value-add to your advertisers. Behind the scenes, Who's Calling technology captures details about every inbound call, tracks the advertisement that targeted it and records the conversation.

National nuances of paid advertisement

Take a look at **http://www.naver.net** (figures 7.5. and 7.6.) and note the four levels of sponsored links:

1st level – Sponsored Link is fed through Overture Korea.
2nd level – Power Link is provided by Naver, and it is below the Sponsored Link from Overture.
3th level – Plus Pro is below the Power Link and a website's image can be put here.
4th level – Bizsite is below the Plus Pro.

Figure 7.5. NAVER national PPC

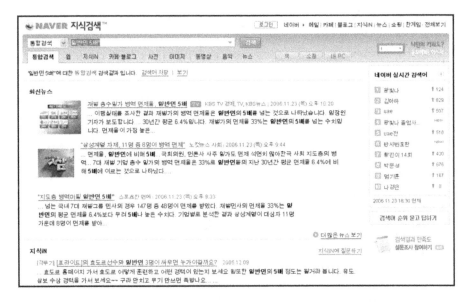

Figure 7.6. NAVER National PPC (4 ad categories)

The first two pages of Naver are devoted to sponsored links, and organic listings only start on the third page. It does not garantee to put any organically submitted website among top 40 results, if both organic and PPC advertisements are shown for the single query together.

Bid Management Tools

Many vendors provide software and services that help automate paid placement bidding and reporting for you.

Most popular, with integrated tracking across 30+ search engines, is Atlas Search **http://www.atlasonepoint.com**. Atlas Search tracks buys across top search engines, including Google, Yahoo! (Overture), Miva, Ask Jeeves, Mirago and more. Campaign optimization automatically manages groups of keywords according to metrics you specify, such as return on advertising spend, cost per acquisition, sales and net revenue. Bid rules return on advertising spending (ROAS) and return of investment (ROI).

Indextools **www.indextools.com** offers live cost analysis that makes expense tracking on paid search engines (including Google, Overture, Miva, Lycos and more) easy by showing ROAS in real time for each distinct keyword and search phrase. Index Tools Web Analytics 9 analyzes your search engine performance, identifies your most popular pages and entry points, and improves website navigation and usabilty. API integration enables you to interface with Indextools proprietary database and functionality through SOAP/XML.

At the SES 2006 Conference in NY, a European bid managemnet platform **http://www.holosfind.com** (formerly **www.referencement.com**) has been presented. It allows for managing multiple search engines and PPC networks under one multilingual platform (French, Spanish, and Italian). It supports trusted feed programs including Syndicaton Yahoo!, Overture, Wanadoo, Voila.fr. Their exclusive technology is Java-based, and the data exchange is done in different formats (XML among others), reporting is real time.

7.2. Direct Advertisement

In the Internet jungle, you can set up traps for your prey on any online property that allows it. There are many types of feeds, direct mailing, banners, scrapers, traps, like pop-ups, etc.

Blogs, Forums & Newsgroup Advertising

Clearly as RSS increases in popularity, publishers will be looking for ways to profit on their content. RSS in advertising is a logical step, and as long they strike the balance between quality, consistent content and occasional related advertisements, advertising in RSS feeds will be successful. Once the balance is lost, publishers may be forced to move to a subscription RSS feed model.

Google's AdSense for Feeds offers contextually targeted advertisements, with a wide selection of advertisers. Google chooses not to reveal the percentage of revenue that is shared with the publisher, so it is difficult if not impossible to predict monthly revenue. While this system was in the beta testing mode, they offered public access and registration, and any blogmaster could integrate AdSense feeds in their blog. Now this system is closed, supposedly to open to public access as a stable service soon.

Pheedo (**www.pheedo.com**) displays categorized advertisements rather than contextual advertisements. The upside to this is that Pheedo's advertisements can be used in conjunction with Google AdSense or AdSense for feeds without violating Google's contract. Pheedo works with the publisher to serve advertisements from similar or related categories associated with the feed's content.

Pheedo's system allows for advanced ad filtering, giving publishers control over keyword ad filtering, specific ad filtering or URL filtering. Pheedo's system also allows publishers to sell ads to existing advertisers with whom they already have a relationship.

Banners & Scrapers Advertising

A banner ad is simply a special sort of hypertext link, but instead of text the link is displayed as a box containing graphics (usually with textual elements) and sometimes animation. Because of thier graphic element, banner ads are somewhat similar to traditional ads you would see in printed publications such as newspapers or magazines, but it has the added ability to bring a potential customer directly to the advertiser's website. This is something like touching a printed ad and being immediately teleported to the advertiser's store! A banner ad also differs from a print ad in its dynamic capability. It stays in one place on a page, like a magazine ad, but it can present multiple images (including animation) and change appearances in a number of other ways.

Like print ads, banner ads come in a variety of shapes and sizes. The Internet Advertising Bureau (**http://www.iab.net**) specifies eight different banner sizes, according to *pixel* dimensions. A pixel is the smallest unit of color used to make up images on a computer or television screen. The full banner (468 pixels wide and 60 pixels high) is by far the most popular, but you will see all these variations all over the web. These are not the only banner ad shapes and sizes, either, but they are a good representation of the range of common banner ads. There is not a universal file size constraint on banner ads, but most websites impose their own limits, usually something like 12 Kilobytes to 16 Kilobytes. This is because banner ads add to the total file size of the page they appear on, therefore increasing the time it takes for a browser to load that page.

Actual graphic content, or *creative*, varies considerably among banner ads. The simplest banner ad features only one, static GIF or JPEG image that links to the advertiser's homepage. More common is the GIF-animated banner ad, which displays several different images in succession, sometimes to create the effect of animated motion. Then there are *rich media* banner ads — ads that use audio, video or Java and Shockwave programming. These banner ads, which usually have larger file sizes, are often interactive beyond their simple linking function.

Banners are not particularly effective compared to PPC and organic advertising. Also, it seems that more and more people simply ignore them while browsing because banners were overused in the past. Internet users have become so accustomed to seeing banners that the presence of a banner does not register in surfers' minds as it once did.[24]

Scrapers are online ads significantly larger than the 120x240 vertical banners, with heights often ranging from 500 to 800 pixels (and widths often ranging from 120 to 160 pixels)[25]. For a long time there weren't any standard sizes to which buyers and sellers adhered. This made scrapers the province of large, well-branded sites that could sell custom advertising packages.

The IAB has since announced standard sizes for scraper ads. The standard scraper is 120x600 and wide scrapers are 160x600. With standards in place, scraper ads have become more common in advertising networks.[26]

Pop-ups are another form of advertisement. These are considered very annoying as they appear in a new window while you are browsing. Most people do not pay attention to pop-ups and close the window before it even downloads completely. Many Internet surfers use pop-up blocking software to avoid receiving them altogether.

There's an alternative to pop-up called pop-under. It serves the ad in a window that loads behind the main website window, so the ad is actually seen only when the main window is closed.

Claria (**http://www.claria.com**) develops and distributes ad-serving software that presents users with pop-ups and pop-unders whenever they visit specific websites. Claria (the former Gator, or Gain AdServer) network adds cookies to your computer to push targeted content to users. Claria and other software of the kind belong to adware that usually comes

---

[24]   BannersXChange.com – a free banner exchange advertising network garantees to triple your click-throughs by making banners immediately visible with no other banners competing on the pages.

[25]   Looksmart's vortals allow advertisers to reach relevant audiences through banners such as Leaderboard (728*90), Rectangle (300*250) or Wide Skyscraper (160*600).

[26]   Some notes about the Spanish market: Terra.com recommends size of banners 468 x 60 (to Forex site) or 728 x 90 (to Sports sites) and size of skyscrapers 728 x 90 (Forex) or 160 x 600 (Sports).
Yahoo! Mexico offers 2 options for banner pricing:
Option1> $3,200 the banner can be seen 4 times/month during 3 hours.
Option2> $6,400 the banner can be seen 4 times/month during 6 hours or 3 hours twice a week during 1 month. Inside a category in Yahoo! Mexico, the quote is a minimum of $2,000 which makes 200,000 impressions. They don't work with skyscrapers.

with freeware programs. There have been a number of lawsuits against Claria, claiming that Claria's software violates various state and federal laws by foisting their rivals' ads onto their sites. However, the company is prospering and the software is still popular among advertisers.

Direct Mail Advertisement

Figure 7.7. Top Direct Mailing Links[27]

COMPANY	URL
Vertical Response	www.verticalresponse.com
Constant Contact	www.constantcontact.com
Boca Networks	www.bocanetworks.com
Topica	www.topica.com
E-target media (FOR RENT)	www.etargetmedia.com
i-marketing consultants	www.imarketingconsult.com
The information refinery	www.constructionlists.com
Infinite media	www.infinite-media.com
Estrela Marketing Solutions	www.estrelams.com
All Media	www.allmediainc.com
Info USA	www.infousa.com
Name finder lists	www.namefinders.com

Figure 7.8. features Arrowemail, one of the popular direct mail advertisement programs (**www.arrowemail.com**). Though Arrowemail is an easy-to-use service, it is very ineffective when trying it comes to creating dynamic content. If you're looking for something basic this is certainly a good and easy service to use. Arrowemail will allow you to insert as many contacts as you'd like and to divide it into groups (even subgroups), and can export results in Excel or XML format.

---

[27] Average package to buy or rent contains from 10,000 email addresses with price from $0.5-$0.20 to buy and $60-$200 CPM (cost per thousand views) to rent a one time mailing list). Packages may contain over 3 million e-mails depending on topic.

Figure 7.8. Arrowemail Direct Mail Program

More Email Marketing Software and Services

Most desktop email marketing software is designed to help you manage your mailing lists, maintain a subscription center, handle bounced and unsubscribed email addresses, and send personalized messages, newsletters and surveys.

In addition, many packages include some reporting and analytics tools to analyze the open rate, CTR and conversion produced by your email marketing campaign.

Web-based applications like Bronto (**www.bronto.com**), Vertical Response (**www.verticalresponse.com**) and Constant Contact (**www. constantcontact.com**) supply merely the same features. However, their advantage is that the campaigns are sent from their own servers that are whitelisted with major email providers such as AOL and MSN, which minimizes the bounce and spam filtering rates. By using such ASP services, you also save your own SMTP server's bandwidth.

Top ten reviews (**http://www.toptenreviews.com**) presents a list of top-rated email marketing software. The leading positions are held by Email Marketing Director from Arial Software, followed by Group Mail and HandyMailer.

Email Marketing Director (www.arialsoftware.com) has numerous features that will help you create an effective bulk email. You can add anchors, hyperlinks, images, subscripts and other formatting options. The software will display your email in three different modes and you can import HTML pages, starting an impressive campaign. In addition, this software will report on the status of each delivery and on the validity of each email address. Email Marketing Director has everything you need to create a professional email marketing campaign. Import your previously created HTML pages and handle all reporting with ease – these are just two of the many features you'll enjoy with Marketing Director.

Group Mail (www.group-mail.com) is a great program at a budget-friendly price. This complete email marketing package, offered by Infacta Ltd., includes a setup wizard to guide you step-by-step through the setup and installation process so you can easily link this program with your email service and create professional email campaigns. GroupMail has tons of features to help you create an effective email campaign. To begin, just select your server type, DNS or SMTP, then the program wizard will quickly guide you through the setup process.

You can make your email list manually by entering each name or import them from an Excel spreadsheet. Both GroupMail Standard and Professional versions are equipped to handle a list of unlimited email addresses.

GroupMail has all of the basic formatting options like bold, italic, underline, justification, changing font size, color and type.

Additionally, you can manage your account, filter your email list, schedule the delivery of your emails and choose from three different types of message encoding.

HandyMailer (www.handymailer.com) from Bladesoft Corporation is one of the best email marketing programs on the market and is the "TopTenREVIEWS Bronze Award" winner. Even someone new to bulk email marketing will see results as they create effective campaigns with this product.

The only downfall of the software is its limited reporting section. As with many of the other email software programs, you won't know how many recipients received and opened their emails. With this software you can import HTML pages, add sound files, images, file attachments and an unsubscribe link.

The only email creation feature that this product doesn't have is pre-made templates that would make creating bulk emails a bit faster. Other than this, the program has everything that you need to create an effective marketing email.

Estimated CTR for an Email Marketing Campaign

Clickthru rates (CTR) derived from mailing lists may vary from 1% (if you purchase a mailing list, or have your in-house mailing list that was over-mailed or formed through a questionable opt-in process) to 5-15% (for trusted newsletters) .[28]

Doorways

Doorways are mini-sites linked to your main site. Doorways are created around a specific product, service or language. Doorways are advertised separately, and then traffic is accumulated on the main website. This allows you to target audiences for specific keywords and then sell upward once they get to your main website.

Some doorways are redirected to the main site so quickly that the visitor cannot even see the doorway site's content. However, search engines do see the content and index it, so doorways appear in the search engine results for keywords that the visitor will never see on the page. This technique is considered spamming by the search engines and can result in your site being banned by the search engines if you use it.

7.3. Online Public Relations

PR Campaign Overview

Public relations are the keystone for building brand reputation and credibility on the market. Mainly, PR (public relations – don't confuse with PageRank) activity consists in collecting users' testimonials, success stories and case studies for later distribution through website, email or press. However, PR also includes active involvement in discussing your product in forums and – in general – participating in every active discussion and review of your product or service online, with the aim of highlighting its main advantages.

Public relations do not result in sales directly, however you will probably see an increase in sales and conversion rates some time after you start your PR campaign, as brand awareness grows and the knowledge about your product is spread over your target audience through word of mouth (your customers actually recommend your products and services to your prospects and to each other).

---

[28]   For more information on average email CTRs, see http://**www.emaillabs. com**/email_marketing_articles/average_email_click_through_rate.html

The Foundation Element : Customers and End Users

The most powerful ammunition for the PR program is the testimony of satisfied users. PR will interview and qualify users and partners provided by Customer to determine their appropriateness as press references. For merchant advertisers and Vortals profiles, PR will write one-page "user profiles" for press use and will work to secure success stories in computer trades, proper vertical trades and national media (where appropriate).

PR uses the screened, referenceable users to pitch standalone user stories to consumer publications, newspapers and broadcast outlets, to provide user quotes in business press stories and to "dress up" press releases.

Run rate PR

PR managers should conduct all standard, "run rate" PR activities. These are the basics of any PR program: personnel announcements, product reviews, compiling the editorial calendar database and pitching all opportunities, maintaining regular contact with key reporters, guerrilla PR and increasing customer's mindshare with the local press.

Media Kit

If your business does not have a media kit (a set of materials, presentations, images and other information to facilitate the task for your information partners), the PR service or department will create one for you, otherwise it will review it and suggest changes. Its task is also to create documents that will support the media outreach effort and maintain the documents to keep them current with updated messaging and content. A standard media kit may include press releases, a company fact sheet, market overview or situation analysis, technical Q&A, white papers, executive bios, diagrams and photos/bios of spokespeople.

Significant News and Press Releases

Beyond run rate PR are the three categories of significant news: new product announcements, sales wins and new partnerships or alliances. These are commonly done through press releases.

A press release is a public relations announcement issued to the news media and other targeted publications for the purpose of letting the public know of company developments.

For large companies and significant industry achievements, press release distribution is preceded by the process of conveying the details and messages about the new offering to the press through a series of pre-briefings (by phone or face-to-face) before the press release is issued.

Services you can use to distribute your press release

PRWebTM (**www.PRWeb.com**) is one of the major press release distribution companies on the web today. PR Web continues to position itself as an industry leader via its Online Visibility EngineTM (OVETM). The OVE takes advantage of multiple channels to ensure complete success by distributing your news to journalists, online news sites and thousands of other online locations to take your news direct to the public. This is done via PRWeb's distribution to over 100,000 journalists and points of contact, 20,000 Advanced RSS Feeds, Multi-Media distribution via 5,000 Media RSS Feeds (mRSS) and Search Engine Optimization (SEO). This visibility is further enhanced by our highly indexed online archives, distribution technology, news search engine inclusion such as Yahoo! News and PR Web's worldwide news syndication.

Let PRWeb place your news directly in front of the eyes of your audience and help you generate publicity, expert status, brand recognition, loyalty, investment interest, new customers, relevant search traffic and powerful reputation management.[29] PRWeb is the first newswire to integrade press release in the blogsphere.

Zanox, Inc. (**www.zanox.com**) is the global market leader in performance-based multichannel commerce. With its zanox XS platform, the Berlin-based company offers a globally unique marketing solution for effective online and offline sales. Zanox offers its customers a comprehensive strategy including technology, services and an established network of sales partners. The modular zanox XS suite encompasses affiliate marketing and search engine management, as well as recommendation marketing, multichannel sales and customer loyalty. Zanox allows you go global and offers one cental solution to multichannel commerce, including Web, mobile, radio and interactive TV.

---

[29] Notes: We received the following results with out $80 contribution to PRWeb on three campaigns:

ForexVortal.com Press Release was read by 118,172 reporters and picked up by 630.

Multlingual Search and Chat Toolbar Press Release was read by 82,326 reporters and was picked up by 552.GamblingVortal.com Press Release was read by 78,742 reporters and was picked up by 604. PRWeb is easy-to-use, offers excellent customer support, and in the end provides professional results.

www.Business.com is the Web's only search engine and directory service focused exclusively on business. Its mission is to provide business professionals the highest quality search results, making it the easiest and fastest way to fulfill their business needs.

Figure 7.9. PRWeb Public Release Interface

Ad Writing Tips

No matter which search engine you pick, you need to write an appealing ad to get users to click on your link.

SEO copywriting is tricky because you have to satisfy both the search engine and the prospects.

Choosing keywords for PPC is similar to choosing them for your website. It is a balancing act because you need to pick terms that will generate quality traffic, but are not so competitive that you cannot justify the prices you pay for them.

Single words are usually more expensive and too general to generate targeted traffic. Many people feel they simply have to use specific terms. You have to track the terms to see if they are working, even if you are sure that they should do the job.

You should concentrate on the audience you are writing for. Be creative and think of what your prospects envision when looking for your product. Immerse yourself in your audience's point of view, then predict, research and test keywords and phrases you would search for if you were them.

Use a catchy header. You can look at traditional advertisements for your product to get a good idea of what works. Look at magazine titles for tips.

Many search engines highlight search terms in your ad if it matches the query, so by placing the search term in your ad, you can bring more attention to it and improve your click-through rate.

You can get highly targeted traffic by bidding on industry catch phrases of the moment. Sometimes, you can get this traffic cheap because only a few people, if any, generally bid on these terms.

Aiming to be number one is not always the best strategy because many people will do anything to stay on top, and thus will continue to increase their bid. It makes sense to bid a bit lower, so as to achieve optimum return on your advertising dollar. Google AdWords offers an option to automatically optimize your campaign by placing your ad where it will generate most clicks, which is not always the same as the top position.

Also, make sure you link to the exact page where you want the user to end up – not just the home page. Users might give up within seconds if they do not see what they are looking for, and simply leave your site.

7.4. Conversion Rates

With PPC and the like, there are no guarantees. Search engines only drive prey to your hunting scene, but it's up to you to make the kill and close the deal. Therefore, it is important to consider what kind of a success rate you will have when deciding whether it makes sense to pay for your leads. This success rate is commonly referred to as a conversion rate. Conversion rate is the percentage of visitors who take a desired action. In most cases, increasing sales is the ultimate goal. Other actions include membership registrations, newsletter subscriptions, software downloads, or just about any activity beyond simple page browsing.

A high conversion rate depends on several factors, all of which must be satisfactory to yield desired results: the interest level of the visitor, the attractiveness of the offer and the ease of the process. Of course, the interest level of the visitor depends on matching the right visitor with the right place at the right time.

The offer's attractiveness includes its value and the quality of the presentation. It is worth noting that small, impulse items typically have a higher conversion rate than large items.

The visitor's ease of completing the desired action depends on your site's usability, which includes intuitive navigation and fast loading pages. Please see the section on usability for more information.

Typical conversion rates differ according to the type of website: sales (e-commerce), lead generation, and subscription-based.

There is not an industry standard for typical conversion rates, so there are only rules of thumb you can consider. The reason for this is that many companies reporting their average conversion rate aren't measuring their volumes correctly. Many don't have their analytics set up properly, and reporting isn't standardized.

Many retailers measure *shopping cart abandonment*. Lead-generation sites should measure *form abandonment*. Fireclick's data shows that 70 percent of catalog surfers abandon their shopping cart. There are so many ways to improve shopping cart abandonment. One of the most common is showing a progress indicator which highlights the step currently taken by the visitor and shows how many steps there are left, like the one you can see at Amazon:

Figure 7.10. Progress Indicator on Amazon.com

Segmenting your Conversion Rate

The most interesting data usually shows up when you start segmenting conversion rates. You can compare things like the conversion rate of new visitors versus that of repeat visitors and conversion rates of visitors who use your internal search engine versus that of visitors who browse.

Statistics show that there are significant differences in conversion rates by search engine. In 2006, in a report titled "What Converts Search Engine Traffic" (for WebSideStory's StatMarket), researchers found AOL (3.49 percent) and MSN (2.35 percent) to be the top major search engines for overall conversion rates. When they looked at this report segmented by electronics retailers, they found CNET (1.64 percent) and AOL (1.28 percent) to be the top engines. In fashion, AOL (1.87 percent) and Google (1.68 percent) were the leaders.

Unfortunately, the same type of data isn't readily available for lead-generation and self-service sites. We suspect these numbers would be all over the place, based on type of lead, cost of product or service sold, and marketing efforts. When you sell "stuff" online, it's much easier to compare apples to apples. It's not the same when dealing with lead-generation or self-service.

Improving Conversion Rates

The basic approach to improving conversion rates of your site is as follows: measure, experiment with changes, and test the results.

Main Conversion Rates to Be Measured

Regardless of the business model, every website has a wide variety of different conversion rates that can be measured. The most obvious are those leading to the completion of an online purchase process or any other activity. These activities can be divided into two main groups:

- Product purchase
- Lead (online registration, or any collection of user information)

Both of these groups are broad (especially the second one) and have many variations. Furthermore, any product purchase or lead can be broken down to a series of smaller discreet steps (each step with its own conversion). However, several big-picture conversions should be your primary focus in the process of Web analytics. They are:

- Home to purchase
- Special offer to purchase
- Lead generation

Home to Purchase measures the share of your home page visitors that made an order with you.

(Home to Purchase Conversion) = (Orders by Visitors to Home Page) / (Visitors to Home Page)

Usually, the order page is located several clicks away from the first page. Therefore, a user should go through a sequence like (home page) – (product category) – (individual product) – (shopping cart) – (checkout) – (purchase complete).

The Home to Purchase conversion is the broadest of all conversion rates and is a good general benchmark. However, if your site has many products, this measure becomes irrelevant. It is not wise to compare conversion rates of purchasing an iPod Shuffle with that of an 80GB iPod Video. Differences in demand and customer perception may often make conversion rates for different products incomparable.

A variation of Home to Purchase is a Search to Purchase conversion. It is, essentially, a Home to Purchase rate for the sites that rely heavily on internal search results. This rate shows performance of the following sales funnel: (search results) – (product page) – (shopping cart) – (checkout) – (purchase complete).

"How can I improve my conversion?" is probably the most common question from people who own any kind of web business. As we have already noted, there is no unified approach (or, even better, a secret magic pill) for improving conversion. The process is about constant changes (but only one at a time!) and gauging the response. It is extremely important to make small incremental changes to see which of them make a positive difference, which have no effect on your conversion and which harm your performance. There is, however, a certain set of web site elements that need your attention more than others do. These are:

- Calls-to-action
- Registration requirements
- Purchase process advancement indicator

Split Testing

Split testing refers to the process of using several variations of an ad or landing page on a small segment of an audience to see which variant delivers most visits and converts best, and then use this variant in the large-scale campaign that follows.

For instance, you may make several AdWords ads with the same copy but different headlines and direct them to a landing page (or different pages) on your site to measure which headline yields the best results.

Customer and Conversion Tracking

In the above paragraphs we discussed conversion rates and that they need to be measured to be improved. Moreover, if you are paying for your advertisements, you need to know whether your advertising dollar goes as far as you expect.

It is hard to over-estimate the importance of tracking your visitors. If you have a serious online business and have no traffic and conversion statistics in place, you might as well be blind.

Now let's see how traffic to your site is measured:

There are several "big guns" in web analytics software industry. These mostly target medium to large corporate customers, though most of them have solutions for small businesses as well. These services let you approach site access statistics from nearly every imaginable angle:

- WebTrends
- Omniture
- WebSideStory
- CoreMetrics

There are a much larger number of smaller low-cost programs and services, including HitLens, HitWise, HitsLink, OneStat, StatCounter, and ClickTracks. Besides, there's always Google Analytics – the free and quite decent service that Google has made from Urchin after purchasing it.

Figure 7.11. Google Analytics

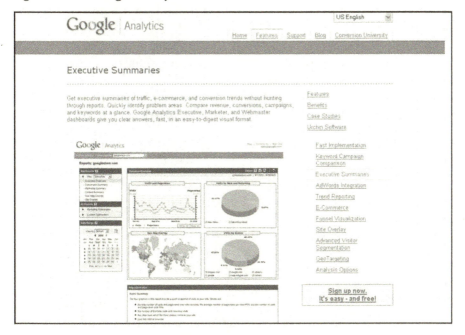

How Analytics Programs Work

There are programs that will pull the stats from your server access logs, and those that will collect real-time statistics by using JavaScript and a remote database. The latter software requires that you insert a special tracking code into each page of your site that you need to track. However, these programs are more popular and provide more exact data, so let's focus on them.

What's in Web Analytics Reports

Web analytics reports contain information that helps you achieve three main goals:

- Correct and streamline your search engine optimization efforts
- Make your site more convenient for human visitors
- Test and optimize your PPC campaigns by switching off underperforming keywords and split-testing the creatives

We will illustrate several analytics reports using HitLens, a visitor tracking solution found in the Web CEO package. It is rather inexpensive and provides a wide variety of reports that are enough for small to medium businesses' marketing intelligence. There are more of them (HitLens includes 100+ reports); we just picked up the most intriguing ones.

Traffic Summary report gives you comprehensive statistics on page views, unique visitors and visits to your site over a period of time.

Figure 7.12. Traffic Summary Report in HitLens/Web CEO

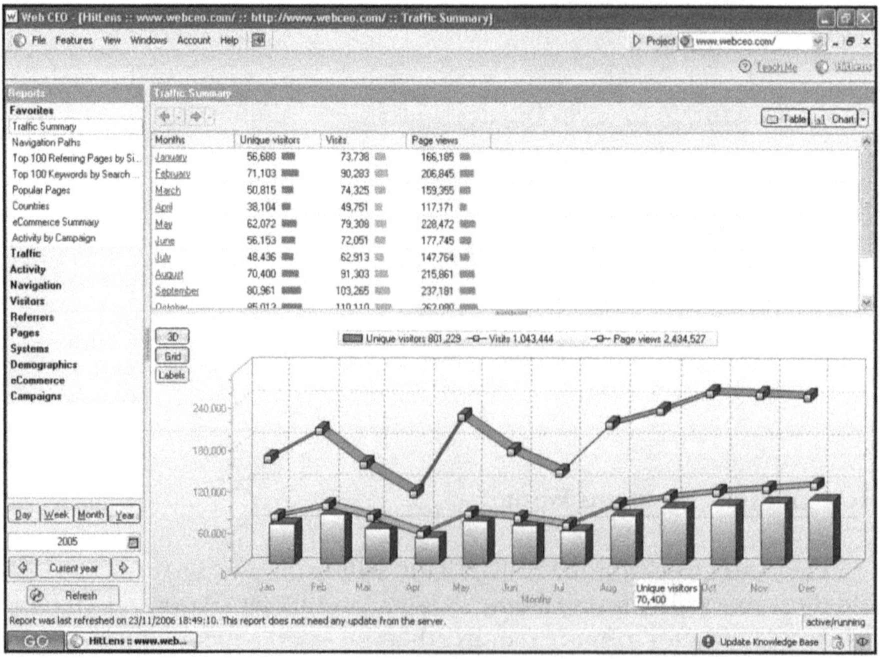

Unique Visitors report shows how many unique visitors entered your site over a period of time – repeated visits made by the same visitors don't count.

Navigation Paths report shows the order in which the pages of your site are accessed. This data may be used to make your site more visitor-friendly.

Entry and Exit Pages report shows which pages are visited first and last (the entry page is the page on your site where the visit begins, and the exit page is where it ends). You should pay special attention to entry pages, as they are responsible for the first impression a visitor receives from your website.

Page and Site Stickiness report tells how long visitors stayed on your site in general and on each single page separately. Use this to understand if your site generates enough motivated interest.

Frequent Visitors report shows how often visitors come to your site. It may help you estimate if your site drives visitors to come back again, or if they only visit once or twice.

Motivated Visits report shows the number of visits when more than one page was viewed.

Visitors by Content Groups shows which content groups attract most visitors (and therefore require the most attention). You define content groups for this report yourself – they may represent such categories of pages as "special offers," "product catalog," "reviews," "news," etc.

Referrers Trends report reveals hourly, daily, and monthly trends in traffic generated by different sources: advertising campaigns, search engines, linking sites, bookmarks, etc.

Referring Sites and Pages report lists all websites and pages that refer traffic to your site. The referring pages are broken down by the domain.

Search Engines and Search Keywords show which search engines and which keywords are good at bringing visitors to your site.

Pages Found on Keywords report is extremely useful, it helps you define which of the pages receive search traffic on certain keywords, and you can optimize those pages accordingly to make them extra relevant for the given keyword.

Popular Pages report lists the pages of your site according to their popularity (the number of visits they've received). Highly trafficked pages are on the top.

Countries, Languages and Time Zones reports show where your visitors come from, in which time zones most your customers live, what languages they speak.

Efficiency of Referrers report shows how many visits and transactions of various kinds (e.g. sales) each traffic source generates. Use this report to compare how different traffic sources (organic results, PPC campaigns, link partners) convert into sales.

Activity by Search Engine/Keyword reports show which search engines and keywords convert best into transactions like sales, leads, opt-ins, etc.

Average Order Size report gives the average order size per referrer. If you have products with different prices, it will help you evaluate if your customers tend to order more or less expensive products and identify the referrer-specific patterns of purchasers' behavior.

First Transaction Cycle Time report shows how much time passes between the first visit and a transaction. You can see how long it may take to convert a visitor into a customer.

Visits before First Transaction report shows how many visits are made before a transaction (e.g. sale) is completed.

Activity by Campaign shows the number of visits, transactions and revenue per advertising campaign.

Cost of Visit by Campaign, Cost of Transaction by Campaign shows how much you spend to acquire a single visitor and a single customer. Along with the ROI, this is the key metric that reflects the profitability of an ad campaign.

ROI stands for "Return on Investment." See how many dollars you spent on advertising came back in sales.

Chapter 8

Global Jungle

As we mentioned in Chapter 1, the proliferation of Internet and growth of technology around the world present the opportunity to reach global markets with previously unforeseen cost efficiency and ease. The global jungle is a vast hunting arena. Expanding your reach to foreign countries takes time and effort, but can make you king of the jungle in the end.

Search Engine Optimization has become one of the most popular and effective forms of marketing available to a global company. According to a recent report, nearly 60 percent of all searches are done in languages other than English[30]. Therefore, optimizing your website for foreign markets can translate into a potentially enormous increase in customer base.

8.1. Globalization Trend

The Internet has made the world a truly global marketplace with millions of prospective consumers. As of March 2008 there are 1,412,489,652

---

[30] Bill Hunt, co-author of "Search Engine Marketing, Inc." Comment quoted from Website Globalization 2005 Conference prospectus

Internet users in the world. This corresponds to a 21.2% penetration rate for the world, based on a total population of 6,676 million. The five-year growth percentage to date is a healthy 165.3%. The Internet is a unique medium because it virtually breaks all barriers of the tangible world, although language is still a significant impediment to international business. (Data taken from **http://www.internetworldstats.com.**)

We can expect the Internet Jungle to double every three years. Therefore, it is increasingly difficult to find your way, similar to *Moore's law*[31]. Just to compare, current information in the Internet Jungle is 500 times more than the information in the Library of Congress, which consists of 19,000,000 books and 56 million manuscripts. The number of websites in June 2008 reached 172 million according to Necraft Survey (**www.netcraft.com**) and growing at a pace of 3.9 million websites a month. This is only the surface of the Jungle. We are not counting blogs, RSS feeds, PR content, books, video and audio content. It is more and more difficult to compete in this enormous environment.

8.2. Second Language Internet in US

Internet usage in the US is still experiencing healthy growth, but with the fast spread of technology throughout the world, the percentage of English-speaking Internet users is declining in the total online market. In 2001, the English-speaking population comprised nearly 41% of all Internet users. In 2005, that number declined to 31%, and will likely decline further in the near future. Please see Figure 8.2.

---

[31]   Moore's Law is the empirical observation that the transistor density of integrated circuits, with respect to minimum component cost, doubles every 24 months. It is attributed to Gordon E. Moore, a co-founder of Intel.

Figure 8.1. Number of Registered Websites in the Internet

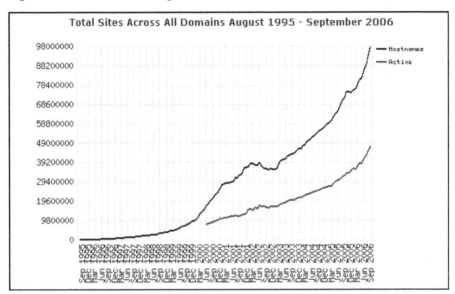

Source: **http://news.netcraft.com/archives/web_server_survey.html**

Figure 8.2. Online Language Populations (Forecast for 2007)[32]

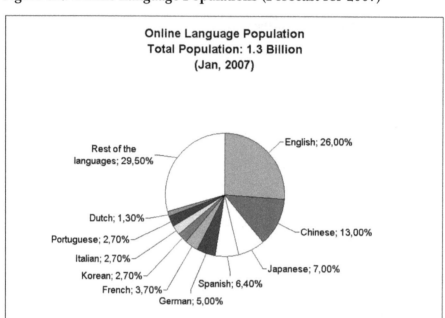

With this great and rapid increase in global Internet usage, the Internet presents an unprecedented opportunity to reach *global* online consumer markets with great cost efficiency and operational ease. Future-oriented companies who want to reap first-mover advantage benefits understand that online marketing is an efficient way to quickly introduce their products to foreign markets.

Besides, the cost of client acquisition in foreign markets is substantially less than in the US because of cheaper advertising prices.

Even if you prefer to keep your business in the US, language-specific SEO still helps you expand your business by allowing you to tap into US ethnic markets.

---

[32]   Universal Engine Group Research (see additional information at Appendix 1) shows us the most popular and growing online languages that are expected to have their own significant share in the near future. Among them are Russian (2005 – 2.38%), Bahasa Indonesia (2005—1.38%), Dutch 1.3% and others.

Figure 8.3. US consumer buying power 1990-2007

	1990	**2000**	2002	2007	**% change 1990-2007**
Hispanic	$223.0	$490.7	$580.5	$926.1	315.3%
Non-Hispanic	$4,054.2	$6,534.6	$7,052.1	$8,944.0	120.6%

There are also tourists and foreign students residing in the US, who search the Internet in their own language. Therefore, multilingual markets are valuable to US-centric firms.

The Internet Jungle describes how to adapt your site to international markets, and how to advertise globally. However, before you decide to expand your business internationally, research market conditions and competition extensively.

8.3. Invisible Jungle

In addition to websites, there is an enormous invisible part of the Jungle, which consists of hundreds times more information than the visible part (See **http://www.brightplanet.com**). The invisible Jungle consists of traditional databases (patents, medical resources, financial resources, different public resources, newspaper classifieds, chats, libraries, different PDF files). For example, all the CNN news is available online, but not ranked by Google or Google cannot be indexed by Yahoo! According to Alexa, more than half of Internet traffic is received by sites in Asian languages, not counting the Chinese websites that are in simplified Chinese (Republic of China) or Traditional (Taiwan, Hong Kong, Singapore). It is possible to say that popular Asian search Engines like Baidu, Sina, Sohu, 163, QQ, Naver, etc. are also invisible for most of the Internet Engish-speaking users.

The trend of foreign language population is exploding on the Internet, where 11 out of 20 sites are **non-American English sites on Feb. 2005** and the figures are still growing.

Figure 8.4. The Top-ranking websites by Alexa.com

Rank	February 2005		February 2006	
	Website	Language	Website	Language
1	www.yahoo.com	English	www.yahoo.com	English
2	www.msn.com	English	www.msn.com	English
3	www.google.com	English	www.google.com	English
4	www.sina.com.cn	Chinese Simplified	www.baidu.com	Chinese Simplified
5	www.passport.net	English	www.yahoo.co.jp	Japanese
6	www.sohu.com	Chinese Simplified	www.sina.com.cn	Chinese Simplified
7	www.baidu.com	Chinese Simplified	www.ebay.com	English
8	www.163.com	Chinese Simplified	www.sohu.com	Chinese Simplified
9	www.yahoo.co.jp	Japanese	www.163.com	Chinese Simplified
10	www.microsoft.com	English	www.passport.net	English
11	www.ebay.com	English	www.qq.com	Chinese Simplified
12	www.3721.c0m	Chinese Simplified	www.amazon.com	English
13	www.qq.com	Chinese Simplified	www.myspace.com	English
14	Offeroptimizer.com	English	www.microsoft.com	English
15	Newsgroup.com.hk	Traditional Chinese	www.yahoo.com.cn	Chinese Simplified
16	Duam,net	Korean	www.google.co.uk	English/UK
17	Tom.com	Chinese Simplified	www.google.co.jp	Japanese
18	AOL.com	English	www.taobao.com	Chinese Simplified
19	www.naver.com	Korean	www.naver.com	Korean
20	Fastlink.com	English	www.bbc.co.uk	English/UK

Source: **http://www.alexa.com/site/ds/top_sites?ts_mode=global&lang=none**

8.4. Internationalization and Localization

The driving force of the Internet is providing the opportunity for businesses and consumers alike to expand their borders of knowledge and increase global interaction. With the worldwide online population continuing to grow, this demand for information will only increase. Within this report, the means of human translation and machine translation are explained and explored. The increasing growth of the Internet, e-commerce expansion and rising volumes of web content will all drive the growth of the industry. The fastest growing segment of this market according to Allied Business Intelligence (ABI) will be for website localization, which has grown in revenues to $3.1 billion in 2007.

According to the "Language translation, Localization and Globalization: World Market Forecasts. Industry Drivers and eSolutions" report, by the end of 2007 the worldwide human translation market was projected to account for $11.5 billion and the machine translation for $134 million of this growing marketplace. The software and web localization markets will respectively account for $3.4 billion and $3.1 billion by 2007 (DATA RESOURCES, Inc. – **http://www.dri.co.jp**).

Globalizing your Website will include two major steps: internationalization and localization.

Internationalization involves restructuring the software used by your e-business so that it can process foreign languages, currencies, date formats and other variations in conducting business globally.

Language encoding

To accept and process orders in Spanish or Chinese, your database will have to be restructured to accommodate those languages. International software usually is compatible with Unicode and international computing standards.

Unicode (**www.unicode.org**) is an encoding system that represents all possible symbols from all world alphabets in a single code table, and even reserves some room for undiscovered ancient languages and custom use.

Unicode has three main variants: UTF-8, UTF-16 and UTF-32. (UTF stands for Unicode Transformation Format).

UTF-8 encodes every possible character using 8 bits. (One bit is either 0 or 1, so 8 bits give room for 256 different combinations like 10010110, 00011010 etc.). Latin alphabet, numbers and punctuation are within this range; moreover, the codes for the first 128 characters are equal to those in ASCII, which makes UTF-8 backward compatible with the pages written in the Western European charset. This means that such pages can be translated into Unicode by just changing the page charset declaration to UTF-8 and nothing else!

Whenever UTF-8 meets a symbol that's not within the first 256 code points (e.g. a Chinese hieroglyph), it uses 16, 24 or 32 bits to encode it. That's why UTF-8 is called a variable-length Unicode format: when you are given a binary representation of a UTF-8 string and are told to split it into characters, you don't know beforehand how many bytes each character takes. However, this approach saves memory because most popular characters occupy less space.

UTF-16 uses 2 bytes (16 bits) to encode popular and not so popular symbols (65536 characters in total, including Chinese, Japanese and Korean alphabets), and reserves 3 and 4 byte combinations for very rare and ancient symbols. However, it is also a variable-length format, a compromise between memory saving and processing ease purposes.

Finally, UTF-32 uses 32 bits (4 bytes) to encode whatever symbol. Software easily and quickly processes UTF-32 strings because it knows every 4 bytes represent another character. UTF-32 is a fixed-length format.

Unicode enables your system to handle iconic Asian Languages such as Chinese, Japanese or Korean. All popular browsers have excellent support for Unicode; however, not all server-side programming languages easily deal with it. For instance, Unicode is well integrated into Java, but PHP will have native support only since version 6 (which was still in development when this was written).

Internet Explorer has support for 7 European encodings (Baltic, Western and Central), 5 Cyrillic, 4 Arabic and Hebrew, and 3 Japanese and Korean. Special attention should be given to Chinese, since it can be written in either the Simplified (GB2312 or HZ) or Traditional (Big5) version. You should consider this when receiving or advertising services in the Republic of China or in Hong Kong, Singapore, Taiwan.

Problems can appear if your web page is given to the browser in a different format than it is declared to be (i.e. you tell the browser that your page is Unicode, but the page is actually encoded as Windows-1252). Such a page or email becomes an unrecognizable sequence of characters in the browser or email client. Whenever you see evidence of such confusion on other websites, try switching your browser to a different codepage; first try those types that the website is most likely to use.

Other sorts of problems are due to incorrect or incomplete conversion between two different encodings (symbols that could not be converted into the target encoding are displayed as question marks).

It is clear that the search machine should be able to recognize the encoding used by a site which it indexes and also the encoding of the query made by the user. But NOT all foreign search systems are able to do so, thus it is better to communicate with them in English.

Localization includes translation and cultural adaptation of your site's content and presentation. A variety of translation options is available for companies with different expectations and budgets, but the most convenient choice is using translation (dump) tools.

8.5. Language Tools

Altavista Babelfish (http://babelfish.altavista.com) – based on the Systran Technology, the oldest and best translation tool. It offers free online translation of texts of up to 150 words into main European languages.

Free Translator (http://www.freetranslation.com) – EU languages free translator

PROMT Ltd (http://www.online-translator.com) – a popular Russian-European language online translator

Worldlingo (http://www.worldlingo.com) – Used in the Microsoft Office Word translator

One Look Dictionary (http://www.onelook.com) – A search engine for words and phrases: If you have a word for which you'd like a definition or translation, OneLook will quickly shuttle you to the web-based dictionaries that define or translate that word. No word is too obscure; more than six million words from over 1,000 online dictionaries are indexed by the OneLook® search engine. Words definition service is powered by Dictionary.com (**www.dictionary.com**).

If you wish to understand the meaning of websites written in other languages, the following language translators will do the job:

http://www2.etown.edu/vl/forlange.html – free-to-use machine translation on the web
http://www.translatorsbase.com/ – free human translation service
http://www.systransoft.com/
http://www.systranet.com – the Systran site
http://www.babylon.com/
http://www.reverso.net/textonly/default_ie.asp
http://www.alphaworks.ibm.com/aw.nsf/html/mt – an online machine translation from Alpha Works at IBM

http://www.translatum.gr/dics/mt.htm
http://www.foreignword.com – provides access to various computer-assisted translation tools
http://www.word2word.com/free.html – gives access to various machine translation engines
http://anglahindi.iitk.ac.in/ – English to Hindi Machine Aided Translation System; an ongoing project at IIT Kanpur, India
http://www.tranexp.com/InterTran/FreeTranslation.html – supports many languages

Google Translation Tool

Google offers several language tools. They are available by clicking the "Language Tools" link on the home page or directly at **http://www.google.com/language_tools?hl=en**. When you enter a search and see that some search results aren't in your language, you can click "translate this page" next to their titles. You will receive a translated version of the page in a separate frame.

Figure 8.5. Google Language Tool

UEG Translation Tool

Universal Engine Group (UEG) Multilingual Toolbar allows users to search in over hundred search engines worldwide, using Multilingual Search, or users can use a dropdown menu to select Google, Yahoo! or MSN as their search engine. Users now have the ability to search in different supported languages, as well as translate search terms to find what they're looking for in different countries or right in their own backyards. Universal Engine Group has incorporated a speaking search engine into its toolbar, so now users will not only be able to translate text-to-text but translate *text-to-voice* and hear their translations as they occur. A Multilingual Chat is also incorporated into the toolbar, which enables users to chat in multiple languages to foreign friends or colleagues, writing in their native language, via real-time translation. Toolbar guarantees to power your search by taking users as locally or globally as necessary. You can download this toolbar at **http://www.download.com/3000-20-10429595.html**.

Universal Engine's Toolbar includes multilingual chat communication, which enables users to chat in all major language-to-language options, including most popular European and Asian languages, via their native tongue by simply selecting a language they would like to speak.

Increasing the amount of visitors is one of the priorities of any website. Manual translation of your web pages could bring you significant additional traffic from foreign markets. However, maintenance on a regular basis – of news, press releases and dynamic content pages, for example – is not possible without machine translation involved.

Installation of special programs that translate your web pages "on the fly" into the language that your visitors choose keeps your site gaining maximum traffic 24/7 without the need to reference a special customer support site. UEG has developed many utilities for the machine translation, including sites translators, multilingual chat, conference and live support in different languages.

8.6. How to Market Globally

Increasing your customer base by increasing visitor flow from overseas is not that easy. Before you can make friends with the creatures of the Global Jungle, you have to learn to speak their language. Language is one of the last barriers on the Internet, so localizing your website starts from making the content of your website comprehensible to the foreign public. Straight translation rarely works because people perceive things and communicate differently across the globe. Therefore, you need to consider what kind of a message you want to convey to your foreign audience and what cultural aspects should be considered in your website's content and design. There are many nuances, like layout, color, style, tone, structure, context, etc. My main advice here is to research all these aspects before you start devoting funds and effort to building and marketing your language site to avoid unnecessary costs and delays.

When you approach localization, the first thing you need to decide is whether you want an international or a truly local website. Each option has its benefits. An international website is composed so that it appeals to anyone in the world. This way you can reach a wide audience. Unfortunately, this also means that you have to strip the site of any cultural affiliation at all, so it is not particularly attractive to a person of any single nation.

On the other hand, you can make your site highly localized by using the design and language style of the particular region. This might narrow your target audience, but at the same time, localized sites send a message of cultural awareness to the visitors, compelling them to do business with you. Localizing your website can be highly effective in terms of conversion, but you need to put in time and effort in order to reap the benefits of a truly localized site. So, unless you are committed to the process of localization, you should play it safe and stick to neutral design and content.

Language Content

As we said before, content is crucial for any website, and generally determines whether a website will be successful of not. When writing for your website you should consider the audience's background and whether offering other languages on your website can benefit them. For example, many websites within the US attract Hispanic users by offering Spanish versions of the website. Hispanics are the largest bilingual population in the US, and they are increasingly becoming desired customers as their income and education levels grow. But when localizing websites for Hispanic users, many people forget that the target is not just users who speak Spanish, but they are US Hispanics. This means that the audience is more likely to use English words for certain phrases.

The same applies to other ethnic groups within a certain nation because these groups develop specific dialects that combine their native language and the language of the country of residence. For example, the combination of English and Spanish is known as Spanglish, and the combination of English and Russian is called Runglish. There's also Chinglish and others; you get the point. Therefore, if you are designing a site specifically for the US Hispanic population, it is important to understand that the audience would appreciate a site geared at the Hispanic audience, but would not require a site written completely in Spanish.

It is hard enough to write compelling copy in English, but when it comes to creating content for your language site the task becomes much more difficult. A simple translation of your website rarely works because people of other cultures relate things differently. Apart from translation technicalities, you must consider the dialect of your target market. For example, there is a substantial difference in Spanish used in the US, in Spain, and in Latin America. Therefore, always think of exactly whom you want to attract before you create a language site.

If you want to create a single site with multiple languages, you need to create source text that would work effectively in any language and market. This means that you need to keep it clear and simple, and avoid as many cultural references as possible. The source text should be coherent and unambiguous. It should conform to any in-house corporate guidelines for terminology and style to reinforce corporate branding, but should also be acceptable to local markets from an idiomatic perspective.

Below are some content creation tips for creating a source text that can be used internationally. This will minimize localization cost and time, and allow the user to read and understand the text easily.

- Keep copy short and succinct
- Write clearly and unambiguously
- Decide upon an appropriate tone of voice and register for the target audience, then stick to it
- Develop and approve key messages and terminology first
- Avoid clichés, cultural references and jargon because they are difficult to translate effectively
- Do not use "street" language or words and phrases that will only be used by a minority of your target audience
- Either avoid abbreviations and acronyms or write the terms out in full before using the abbreviations and acronyms
- Avoid names based on abbreviations
- Even when abbreviations are universally recognized, they can present pronunciation problems for different cultures
- Avoid metaphors or names based on images. A *bull market* or *Groundhog Day* will be meaningless to many cultures
- Be aware that humor often does not travel beyond its culture of origin and can be very expensive to adapt

Since the globalization process is often based on the adaptation of copy and design from an original marketing tool such as an English language website or an advertising campaign, the way in which the original design is created has a substantial impact on localization. When designing for an international marketplace, you have to consider both the cultural and the technical implications – that is, the suitability of the design for local markets and the suitability of the design for the localization process.

A quick note on translating: Do not hire a Belgian to translate your site into Dutch if Holland is your target country. Dutch visitors will notice the difference and dislike it.

An interesting point about Belgians and Flemish – we have seen a lot of evidence of Belgian Flemish speakers viewing Dutch sites. If you want more evidence of this Jorge, ask your Dutch national what region he or she is from and what the difference is between northern and southern dialects. The Dutch person we know is from Amsterdam, and we are told there is a radio show in Holland with the sole purpose of poking fun at Belgians and the way in which they speak Dutch (which is, however, still correct). We understand Belgians are more inclined to visit a Dutch site than the other way around, so a Dutch site may be more beneficial to you.

Cultural Aspects

Producing cultural appeal on your website is not an easy task. It is not only what people of the culture like that have to be considered, but also what the culture dislikes and fears.

People of every nation of the world have their own unique set of beliefs that dictate how they react to what they see on the net. People's attitudes diverge and overlap at the same time, so it is difficult to simply categorize cultural aspects by nation. Therefore, we assembled some examples that will give you a feel for what to expect.

Color and imagery selection is commonly the most difficult task in designing a site for international markets because all cultures differ in how certain colors and images are perceived. Let's take a look:

Color

Color can have a strong positive or negative representation in all cultures. Understanding the impact of color will help with the design, enabling you to emphasize or de-emphasize corporate colors for a global audience.

The color black, for example, signifies death in the West, but in China the color of death is white. Purple signifies bravery and royalty in the West, but is the color of mourning in Brazil. Red is commonly associated with danger in the West but is associated with weddings in China. Green and light blue are regarded as sacred colors in the Middle East, and saffron yellow is a sacred color for Buddhists.

Still, you need not limit yourself to only neutral colors when designing your multi-cultural site. Just make sure you consider your color selection in relation to your target audience early in site development.

Imagery

You also need to be aware of the suitability of images for a global audience and be prepared to offer different images depending on the target market.

Here are some examples of the types of images that can cause difficulties:

People. Many cultures are extremely sensitive to ethnicity, dress and poses, particularly relating to women. A recent poster campaign for Lux, featuring Sarah Jessica Parker in a sleeveless dress, had to be hastily airbrushed to cover her arms for the Israeli market.

Animals. Animals evoke various associations in different cultures. Dogs are generally considered to be man's best friend in the West, but Arab cultures find them unclean and offensive.

Flags. Flags are always best avoided because they are more political than cultural and do not clearly represent a specific language. Which language is represented, for instance, by the Swiss or Belgian flag? However, many people realize that websites use flags as a tool to represent a certain language simply because it is convenient. Still, it is better to be neutral when using flags.

Icons. Common cultural references such as mailboxes, rubbish bins and phone boxes are often used in website designs but are unlikely to be universally understood as each country has a different design.

- In Spain patriotic symbols are generally disliked due to historical reasons. The flag was overused by the 40-year dictatorship, and unfortunately the excessive use of flags by any country is related to fascism and lack of freedom. We know this occurs in other European countries where the use of flags is construed as manipulation.
- If you are an American company trying to sell in Europe, be aware that the Clinton credits are depleted. BUT the negative image

of America now does not have to be an impediment to business. American business still enjoys an image of quality, seriousness and effectiveness. You can hear in the same sentence someone complaining about Americans while stating their products are the best. So keep your site non-political and strictly professional.

- Europeans have a thing with complaining about their neighbors; We guess it is the history of the continent. Every country seems to have invaded the rest at one point or another. If you think this is silly just think about the confederate flag and the problems it sometimes brings. As for its application to web localization, try to avoid it. French may be spoken in several countries in Europe, but is it worth offending other countries to use a French flag as the French language indicator? The same goes for German, Italian, Dutch, etc . . . .

Technical Aspects

Besides color and imagery, you need to make sure your website is ready for internationalization from a technical perspective. There are a number of issues here; let's take a look:

Text Expansion

No two languages take up the same amount of space when laid out in a design. Individual words can expand by up to 300%, and design elements such as a text box can sometimes take up twice as much space as the English source. But one paragraph in a document might expand by 30%, and the next may not expand at all. Some languages such as Russian can expand up to 70%. Others such as Hebrew and Asia-Pacific languages may contract and take up less space.

Therefore, in sites with multiple languages, you need to consider how to accommodate text expansion in your design. The layout and design of the original must either allow space for such expansion to occur or for elements to be moved. Generally, text expansion is handled by expanding into empty areas of the page or by reducing the size, leading and tracking of the text (by as little as possible). In some cases, however, more deliberate action must be taken. For example, headlines often do not translate easily, and five words can become eight or ten. Point size reduction is often the only option in a design where text expansion has not been taken into consideration. Interesting alignments and typographical emphasis of the different elements of a headline can, as a result, be difficult to reproduce.

Captions should not be crammed too tightly on a page, either to a graphic or to each other. A heavily labeled diagram needs plenty of space for text expansion.

Tables and forms are difficult to handle because of the use of unalterable colored backgrounds and lines that make expansion impossible.

Fonts

Non-western languages require different typefaces in order to have room for the extra characters not supported by standard fonts. It is, therefore, a good idea to consider what languages will be required at the earliest possible stage of design before you decide on which font you are going to use. If you want to use a particular font across all your communications, remember that the font should be widely available in all mediums.

For website localization, Arial and Times New Roman are probably the safest bets. If a browser cannot display the correct font, the result will be the nearest approximation the browser can find on the machine, which may compromise the design.

There are mainly three types of fonts: serif, sans-serif and monospaced. Whether a user's browser will or not be able to display your text depends on whether the font you've declared for it is available on their computer. For this reason, try using fonts that are supplied with the Windows operating system. Windows sans-serif fonts are Verdana, Arial, Arial Narrow, Tahoma, Microsoft Sans Serif, Century Gothic, Trebuchet MS and others. Windows serif fonts are Times New Roman, Georgia, Book Antiqua, Bookman Old Style. The most popular monospace font is Courier. These are present on all Windows computers and are safe to use on Web pages.

Corporate Fonts

Unless they have been developed by large organizations with large budgets, corporate fonts tend not to support non-English characters. Font design and creation are highly specialized and expensive processes.

Where a font is used that does not support localized characters, the only option is to find the closest available match for the target character set, which means that your agencies and localization companies must also possess a copy of the chosen font. It is possible to produce customized versions of Western European fonts for non-western languages, but it means that extra time will have to be built into the project. In short, failing to carefully consider font selection at the design stage can add time and cost to a project.

Default Font Alternative

CSS (cascading style sheets) used to make up the page's style provide the ability of specifying several fonts in one declaration, so that if the browser does not find the first font it will try the second, etc.

The following CSS rule:

font-family:Verdana,Arial,Helvetica,sans-serif;

tells the browser to use Verdana font to display the text; if the Verdana is not available, Arial will be used; if both Verdana and Arial are absent, the browser will try Helvetica; and finally, if none of the three fonts is found, the browser will try the system default sans-serif font.

Designing for Bidirectional and Double-byte Languages

Bidirectional languages such as Arabic and Hebrew may require a full re-working, as they must read from right to left. This means the production of reversed artwork and possibly a change of graphics.

Consultation at the earliest possible stage of design will assist with speedy delivery of localized Hebrew and Arabic versions.

While some publishing packages readily support the direct input of Asia-Pacific character sets such as Chinese, Japanese and Korean, localized design can be produced so that the file can be run through the normal printing process without the need for specialist software. Again, our advice is to consult with the experts at the earliest possible stage of design to ensure the speedy delivery of localized Asia-Pacific versions.

Avoid Turning Text into Graphics

The guiding principle is to avoid putting translatable text elements in separate graphics files unnecessarily – either for online or offline communication. Once embedded into a graphics file, it is a manual process to extract the text, and this has to be done separately from the main text extraction. A better approach when designing for print is to place text in frames laid over the graphic. This means that text can be extracted in one simple process. Less switching between programs is needed during the typesetting process, and there are fewer files to deliver once localization is completed. It is easier to accommodate different graphics for different language versions as appropriate without involving translators and typesetters in the process. Burning text into graphics for online communication means that it is displayed in a certain way and cannot be adjusted by user screen resolution preferences or the re-sizing of a window. This might be desirable from a design perspective, but it makes the localization process longer and more complex because there is no efficient way of automating text extraction and re-insertion into graphics, and you will probably need to involve a DTP/web graphics specialist. The same look and feel can often be achieved using plain HTML, particularly with the use of Cascading Style Sheets, and this process results in a far more localization-friendly design.

Embedding text in graphics also makes your design suitable only for the English language. If text is already embedded, ensure that the design allows for language expansion. Otherwise, the only option for localized versions is to reduce the point size to make the text fit, and this can affect the legibility of the content.

Preparing for international departures is not difficult, but it does involve getting a grip on a number of cultural issues before you even brief your creative agency. You need to work with a partner who understands internationalization and localization; otherwise you could make costly mistakes.

Never underestimate the potential sensitivity of any ethnic, religious or cultural group to what you say and to how you present your business visually. As any business knows, a reputation can take a lifetime to earn and a moment to destroy. So why jeopardize your chances of international success just because your agency didn't know that a beautiful young Chinese woman dressed in white is more likely to be on her way to her funeral than her wedding?

8.7. Registration and Law

Now you are ready to advertise globally, but take notice of registration laws.

The World Wide Web is still considered "wild west" territory by many because steep rules and regulations are yet to develop. There are basic rules applicable to the entire web, but Internet laws in every country are different. The differences are especially pronounced in policies towards gambling and pornography, so be extra careful if you are in one of these businesses.

In the Jungle, when you enter someone else's territory, you have to know and abide by local laws in order to keep the peace. Even in less-developed online markets it is worth it to follow the rules even if there is little enforcement since establishing a good reputation serves you well in any part of the world.

Becoming well-known globally starts with establishing a local online presence. First, you should register a local website. Since search engines developed separately in each country, many search engines are built to primarily recognize websites with local extensions. So if you have a .com, an international search engine may not pick up your website or would not rank it high. You need to register a country-specific domain if you want search engines to notice it.

When you register, make sure you comply with registration laws. For example, many countries like France require a firm to have a physical presence within the country in order to maintain a local website.

Also, make sure you know the hosting laws, because in some countries hosting must be in the same country as registered site. Because of server delays, you need to host on both sides of the continent if a continent-wide marketing campaign is in place.

As with registering in US, it pays off to pay attention to the Terms & Conditions because otherwise you might run into unexpected expenses. For example, while domain registration might be cheap, changing your DNS might be expensive. So read the fine print and protect yourself against unpleasant surprises.

To register a European domain, we recommend **www. europeandomaincentre.com**. To register Asian domains, we recommend **http://www.asiadns.com**.

Here's an outline of local presence requirements for popular languages:

Figure 8.10. Countries Where Local Presence is Required for Local Domain Names

Domain	Country	Term (Years)	Install	Local Presence
.ar	Argentina	1	inclusive	Required
.com.au	Australia	1	inclusive	Required
.at	Austria	1	inclusive	Required
.be	Belgium	1	inclusive	Required
.br	Brazil	1	inclusive	Local business: required
.bg	Bulgaria	1	inclusive	Required
.ca	Canada	1	inclusive	Required
.cl	Chile	1	inclusive	Not required
.cn	China	1	inclusive	Not required
.cx	Christmas Island	1	inclusive	Not required

.com.co	Columbia	1	inclusive	Required
.fr	France	1	inclusive	Required
.de	Germany	1	inclusive	Required
.gr	Greece	1	inclusive	Required
.hk	Hong Kong	1	inclusive	Required
.is	Iceland	1	inclusive	Local business: required
.in	India	1	inclusive	Required
.ie	Ireland	1	inclusive	National passport: required
.il	Israel	1	inclusive	Not required
.it	Italia	1	inclusive	Business in Europe: required
.jp	Japan	1	inclusive	Required
.kr	Korea	1	inclusive	Site in national language: required
.mx	Mexico	1	inclusive	Not required
.nl	Netherlands	1	inclusive	Required
.co.nz	New Zealand	1	inclusive	Not required
.no	Norway	1	inclusive	Required
.com.pk	Pakistan	1	inclusive	Not required
.com.pa	Panama	1	inclusive	Not required
.com.pe	Peru	1	inclusive	Required
.ph	Philippines	1	inclusive	Not required
.pl	Poland	1	inclusive	Not required
.ro	Romania	1	inclusive	Not required
.ru	Russia	1	inclusive	National passport: required
.sg	Singapore	1	inclusive	Local business: required
.es	Spain	1	inclusive	Required
.se	Sweden	1	inclusive	Local business: required
.ch	Switzerland	1	inclusive	Not required
.com.tw	Taiwan	1	inclusive	Required

.th	Thailand	1	inclusive	Local business: required
.tr	Turkey	1	inclusive	Company or TM: required
.co.uk	United Kingdom	1	inclusive	Not required
.us	United States of America	1	inclusive	Required
.com.uy	Uruguay	1	inclusive	Required
.com.ve	Venezuela	1	inclusive	Not required
.eu	European Union	1	inclusive	Required

8.8. Advertising Style

Advertisements can be aggressive or subtle. The acceptable advertising styles differ across the globe.[33] Examples:

Canadians tend not to like "in-your-face" advertising, and also tend to mistrust implications that you should buy a product because of patriotic reasons (unless it's a patriotic product). The assumption is that you have a substandard product and are trying to sugar-coat it with flag waving. Having said that, an acknowledgment that they *have* a country is always appreciated – how hard is it to leave space for a postal code as well as a zip code? – Especially on sites that ship to Canada. I imagine citizens of other countries dislike ethnocentric behavior as well.

No European country likes the "in-your-face" marketing. Keep it matter-of-fact; dry language is preferred to WHOO HA!!

Be aware of the difference in Spanish, French and Italian between proper treatment and familiar treatment. The word "you" In Spanish is: *tu* (informal) or *usted* (formal), in French *tu* or *vous*, and in Italian *tu* or *Lei*. This is VERY important when writing marketing copy. Don't let a translator make the choice for you. Only if you target teenagers or very "cool" or non-traditional products such as tatoos or body piercings should you use the familiar term. You can compare it to greeting your customers by saying "what's up buddy." This isn't a very good idea if you are selling corporate services, for example. In some parts of these countries people

---

[33] These examples are from **www.searchenginewatch.com**'s multilingual forum. The comments do not necessarily represent the views of this book's authors. We thought that this robust discussion would give you an all-around sense of cultural issues.

don't even use the familiar terms with their own parents. For a more complete description of these formal or polite terms, go to:

http://everything2.com/index.pl?node=tu%20versus%20vous.

The European Union is an economic union, not a cultural union. Although some are closer than others, like Italians and Spaniards, the norm to apply is that they all have their own peculiarities and they do not necessarily like each other. Mentioning that your product is successful in France will not help your Spanish market and the same goes for Holland and Belgium or France and Belgium. In Holland some children's bedtime stories speak of the "spaniards coming to get you if you don't behave," drawing upon clashes from the sixteenth century (as told to me by a Dutch national). People are individuals as well as country nationals and would not often classify themselves as Europeans.

Not to over simplify, but I think you have to be aware of a few facts before going into a new market in Europe.

A recap:

- Be aware of cultural differences in the use of language and the use of proper nouns.
- Patriotic symbols not related to a business may not be perceived well and Flag use can be sensitive.
- American businesses are considered to be very effective and professional; use this to your favor.
- The Internet market is still growing in Europe and is not as commonplace as in the US, so you may need to include a more personalized approach.
- Do not consider Europeans as one entity, they have big cultural differences and in some cases dislikes.

Another factor is Pay-Per-Click – not so popular in Spain, but boy is it rocketing in the UK, Scandinavia, Germany, the Netherlands and France. And it's going to spread! There are European markets where 'search marketing' is incomplete without a PPC element and I think that's going to be increasingly the case.

Which brings up a pet peeve of mine: I work, travel and offer services to the US market for a good portion of my business, my company is incorporated in the US, and most of my friends are American. But it still annoys me to be called an American. This is not because I have a problem with Americans, but because I'm NOT one. I also don't have a problem with men, but I'd prefer not to be referred to as "him," as is commonplace in generalized marketing.

If you decide to offer to a market, offer to the market. Specifically, don't write a page aimed at Americans and assume it will appeal to Canadians. Don't write a page intended for one European country and just assume that the rest will line up to buy your products. Either make the site general enough that nationality isn't particularly an issue, or be VERY specific.

The one problem with this is that, unlike many other countries, Americans really do react well to patriotic branding, and they are a very important market. I hesitate to suggest that an American company avoid an effective marketing tactic for their primary audience just because of other countries' preferences. It works both ways.

My suggestion would be to NOT assume that the US site is your generic "English" site. Rather, make your US site your US site and make a different one for the international English site. Either that, or have only an international English site.

Something else: I have no problem visiting a site I know to be US-centric and seeing that, sure enough, it's US-centric. But a site that purports to be international SHOULD be international, not US-centric. These are two very different things.

I use the US as an example because it's the most obvious example to me in my daily work, but the same applies to other countries as well. I've visited sites based in England and barely understood half the words and phrases in it. I had to actually visit England in order to start understanding some of the slang and local idioms. And I still don't understand any reference to any sporting event.

Which also applies to Americans – leave the baseball and other sports analogies off the site – the rest of the world may not understand idioms like "hitting a home run," "getting to first base," "it's the bottom of the ninth" and so forth.

It's charming if I know it's an English site catering to an English audience. At that point, I'm a "tourist" and accept this as the norm. But If I'm on this site because it's being touted as an international brand or company, then I don't want localized English – I want international English.

The same applies to French, Spanish, Chinese, etc. The language reflects the culture, and the culture reflects the language. If you are trying to promote a culture-neutral website, you need to use culture neutral language.

Don't assume your local site is international just because it's on the web and accessible internationally. There are significant benifits to offering a localized site to visitors, but it comes at the cost of actually doing your homework.

One thing I like to suggest is that you hire (or subcontract) an SEO, writer or designer from the area you are designing for, and listen carefully to what he or she says. Even if you have a talented and capable team of your own, I recommend you bring in an expert on the local area while developing the localized site. Language isn't good enough – you need someone familiar with the culture, too.

While it is agreed that many people would look to outsource copywriting I think with some solid research and an intelligent approach it can be done effectively in-house. The main requirement is intelligence, both in mental capability and thorough background (research) of your audience.

Speaking of Europe as "a sum of many markets with many things in common" and likewise, many unique, here's an interesting article I read a while back that I dug out after following the discussion. It's not about SEO, but it's still relevant. Think global, act European[34].

That's true and it's easier. From my point of view, you've got a few different markets in Europe:

- Northern countries well connected to the Web and good buyers with English sites (Norway, Sweden, Netherlands, UK, Denmark)
- Central countries well-connected to the Web and medium buyers for English sites (France, Belgium, Switzerland, Germany, Spain, Austria, Italy, Greece)
- Central countries well-connected to the Web and good buyers for French sites (France, Belgium, Switzerland)
- Countries who prefers having their own language site (except French & English) tend to be good buyers (Spain, Germany, Portugal, Italy)

Do not make an American wait (he will consider it an insult since his time is valuable).

To a Latino, time has different connotations, as many a long waits in a reception area can prove.

If an Indian tells you that you can call him anytime, he really means it.

The Japanese nod their heads as they listen; it does not mean yes, it means simply that they are listening.

In France the work place is highly structured, and the boss has lots of space.

In an Arab country, the boss will often be found in the middle of a chaotic, small, unimpressive office.

---

[34]   http://www.strategy-business.com/enewsarticle/enews083004?pg=all

An example from a friend: I am a firm believer that I can cater to the differences of every country's manner of addressing one another and possibly double my conversion.

Being Australian in the US, I am always aware of the subtle differences. I watched American shows while growing up in Australia, but the perspective I brought to the viewing was obviously different. I was not living in the culture, just observing it from the commonality of a language. The Brady Bunch became a symbol for the American Dream, of how the US saw life (as bizarre as that seems). If they had made an Australian version the situations may have been the same but the subtle differences would have been the thing that made it Australian: rugby instead of US football, cricket instead of baseball, the father's work environment, the cultures they interacted with, etc. all would have been different. While a US audience might have enjoyed it, they would have seen it as something foreign and not of their own neighborhood. Similarly, the web experience is seen through a national, even ethnic mindset that in most cases we are totally unaware of. Awareness and adaptation to serving these differences is what makes for more successful interaction and thus, better results.

When it comes to purchases, first thing's first: I know of a Spanish bank that still doesn't allow purchases online with their cards, credit or debit. Call centers help, of course, but the reason they're needed is also because they're the quickest way of knowing you'll be heard and given a response. Most companies in Spain don't reply to their customers' emails on a daily basis. And generally speaking, customers calling online stores' calling centers are far more educated than the regular folks calling the brick and mortar store, even if it's the same brand.

What is true in Spain, and I suppose in countries like Portugal and Greece as well, is that most of the online businesses are like a showcase of the brick and mortar stores, or a big catalogue offering exactly the same product or service, but most of the times without the same advantages (you have to wait a median of five or more days to get your product, while going to the store gets you the product instantly, an if it's a supermarket we're talking about, you can see and touch the product), and it's been very recent that the big companies are really considering internet as another business channel, not one of those things we have to have because some consultant says so.

If you're not a branch of a brick and mortar, you choose the way you address your customers according to the target you're targeting (be it *vous* or *tu*). If you're a branch, you use the same language being used in the rest of the group for that area. If the website is intended only for one area or country, then no problem, if it's intended for more than one country, there's almost always a standard language that is understood for most of those language speakers, even if it has to distinquish between Lorries and trucks, computadoras and ordenadores.

Patriotic symbols may be well received if you know who you're addressing. Brits love the Union Jack, and Catalonians love the Senyera. Use of flags in Spain and most of the EU is accepted as a way to indicate language and/or region served, but not as a display of pride except in special cases (like you've won the marathon).

Think global, act local (the HSBC motto) applies. You can't sidestep knowing the locals if you want to succeed. And if your locals think you can be trusted or recognize your brand, you have a big advantage. But you can't go local as iTunes has in Europe, arousing suspicion because of the differences in price for the same product. I think that for an American company, Amazon's approach is much better.

8.9. CRM for the Global Jungle

CRM (Customer Relationship Management) is used to provide an integrated web-based proprietary platform, which enables customers to conduct real-time, cross-lingual and cross-cultural communication.

International promotion strives to offer a broad range of solutions targeting the next generation of information and consumer electronic devices. The aim is to build on our strengths in multilingual mobile devices and to become the leading supplier of language solutions for the wireless industry. The goal is to break language barriers that have hastened the globalization of businesses and take sharing of worldwide information — which is made for most popular languages — into your hands and into your own language.

The answer is CRM – Customer Relationship Management or CMR. Customer Management of Relationships is defined by F. Newell in his book: *Why CRM (Customer Relationship Management) Doesn't Work*, or PM, *Permission Marketing* by Seth Godin, whose blog is one of the most creative on the web.

(http://sethgodin.typepad.com)

CRM allows you to empower customers so they can tell you what kind of information they want, how they want you to communicate with them: where, when and how often. It is a wise solution for businesspeople at all levels, in all industries who want to stay ahead of the curve in the development of customer loyalty.

People in most of Europe are still wary of buying over the Internet. If you couple this with the fact that Mediterranean and many eastern

European countries like to conduct business in person, over a meal or drinks, the Internet becomes a difficult place to conduct business. The solution is to offer a visible telephone number that people can call, or as a second choice, an online chat. People in Europe always call before, during, and after a purchase. It would be funny if it weren't such a support hassle. They simply want to know that there are real people behind your business. It is normal for people calling just to say: "Hi, I just wanted to know if you guys are there. I'll go ahead and buy now," and then call you five minutes later and say: "I bought your product! I hope it is as good as it sounds." I strongly recommend considering phone support for your European markets.

It's very easy to fall into generalizing. This is in fact true sometimes that Europeans are wary of buying over the Internet – and very untrue at others. In the UK, a lot of business is done over the Internet, as well as in Scandinavia.

Figure 8.11. In-language CMR/CMR Support[35]

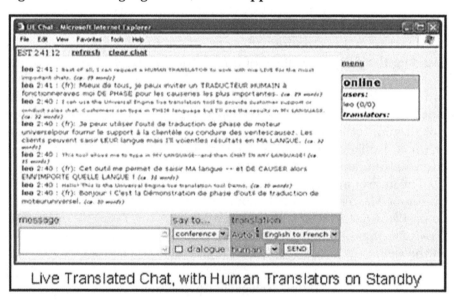

Live Translated Chat, with Human Translators on Standby

As for Internet use, it is widespread in Europe, especially email and search; however, buying is still very low considering the conversion ratio.

---

[35] Many companies offer CMR live product with chat and phone support similar as **www.liveperson.com**, but none gives you the multilingual support as you see at Figure 8.11., except for UEG.

Some of the points we mention above are key in order to understand why Europeans do not buy as much as Americans over the Internet. Another reason, at least in Spain, is how difficult it is to have your bank allow you to use your credit card for online purchases (this also happens in some South American countries). Also we would like to know the difference between cash and credit card purchases in the US compared to Europe. We are sure that also is a factor to consider.

We know that there is an issue with credit cards in Spain – there is in Germany, too – but we believe the penetration and use of credit cards in the UK is one of the highest in the world. The average is something like four credit cards per person which is extremely high, and the rate of growth of online commerce in the UK is greater than in the shops. It's a big business and people are spending.

Regarding purchasing, yes, each and every country has its own particular market with its pros and cons. Credit card usage as well as many other factors can vary broadly. That is why we specified Spain as the country in Europe that we knew of that had problems using credit cards for online purchases; we were not generalizing. Some things can and must be generalized in marketing if you want to be able to target a broad market or any market at all. You have to assume certain factors to be true or you will not be able to create a far-reaching message. This does not mean the generalization applies to every citizen in that country. It means that hopefully it is true for my target audience; let that be segmented by income, sex, race, education, etc. We still don't think we made any assertion that is not basically correct, but rather give some insight to some aspects of the European market. The Internet use in the UK is closer to the US than any other country. The growth is fast because most countries have not reached a peak yet. Once this limit is reached it will grow at a steadier, slower rate. What this tells us is that the growth is largely because there is great room for improvement. In Spain that piece of data is used to manipulate public opinion into thinking the Internet use is growing quickly thanks to state funded initiatives. When you have a two-dollar business and you double that market, your business is growing fast but it still sucks. This is true for Spain, Italy, Greece, Portugal; We are not saying it is for the UK at all. Still we believe the potential is there for all those countries and the rest of Europe, which is why we support the idea of localizing sites for other markets. Even considering the cost, a smart and well-budgeted translation and localization project will be rewarded. This is also true since many European countries do not have a huge Internet market so, on the plus side, there are also fewer companies competing out there.

When you are choosing keywords for your website targeting the Spanish market (340 milion people with 6% Internet penetration) first of all, you have to be aware of where your target is located. There are several Spanish markets that speak different Spanish languages.

Sometimes we think it's enough to translate the keywords from English to French, German, Dutch and Spanish, but it's not enough. Experts' participation yields good results when translating from English to US Spanish, Mexican Spanish, Argentinean Spanish, Spaniard Spanish and more (the same applies to the French language). Nowadays, the marketing success and the SEO require far more than using an e-dictionary to translate.

Keywords you choose to optimize your pages are so important that you generally shouldn't think twice before asking a native speaker to pick the right lingo with the correct words.

US Spanish is very close to Mexican Spanish but is sometimes mixed with English words (it's also called Spanglish, as mentioned earlier). Mexican Spanish, Argentinean Spanish and Spaniard Spanish are really different from each other. Some (only some!) verbs and words have completely different meanings. Argentinean people laugh a lot when speaking with Spaniards and the reason is the verb "coger" (catch in English); In Spain people use this verb to take a taxi, the bus, take the subway, catch a ball, and hold everything. Argentinean people use the verb "agarrar" because in their dialect "coger" is a sexual word. You can imagine the situation when the two are talking.

8.10. International Search Engines

As US companies continue to expand globally, currently employing more than 60 million overseas workers, motivating and rewarding these diverse workforces is a significant challenge to organizations. Managers must be sensitive to differences, since what is acceptable in one culture may be taboo in another one.

For example, in the Hispanic culture family is especially important, so effective recognition might involve someone's family: having an open-house celebration, or family picnic, for instance, or providing some type of reward that can be shared with one's family. The Japanese culture is very group-oriented, so a work group-based form of recognition would have greater impact.

The scope of this book does not allow us to discuss the effectiveness of search engines for each particular country. If you want to have an international presence online, it makes sense to contract a marketing firm that offers global submission. Otherwise, you would need to hire a person within each language group to conduct submission and monitoring, which is very costly.

Here's a list of major search engines by country:

http://www.whitelines.nl/index.html (also provided in the Appendix to this book).

Exalead, an innovative provider of search software designed to simplify all aspects of information access, announced it has indexed more than 4 billion Web pages as part of its commitment to offer customers an easier way to find information on the World Wide Web. Business professionals, consumers, researchers and bloggers around the globe have already recognized the power of Exalead's search-by-serendipity approach. Exalead's unique, unified user interface lets individuals narrow down, refocus or broaden their search queries to explore information in a more natural way.

Exalead's 64-bit technology is incredibly efficient and requires nearly ten times fewer resources to do the job.

The Exalead Web search engine (**www.exalead.com**) was released in October 2005 and serves as the foundation for a company's search software solutions for the desktop, workgroup, enterprise and datacenter. Exalead's mission has always been to provide a unified user interface – from the desktop to the enterprise and the Web – to ensure a consistent search experience. Based on real-time statistical linguistics, statistical semantics and entity extraction technology, Exalead's Web search engine offers a wide range of advanced query capabilities and linguistics features. These include spelling suggestion, phonetic search, fuzzy matching, proximity search, word stemming, search term highlighting, multi-language search, automatic phrase detection and translation. Additionally, Exalead offers personalization options on its home page, shortcuts and personal bookmarks. A smart preview feature lets users browse results with ease.

National Spanish Search Engines

Most popular Spanish national search engines and directories (by **www. alexa.com**):

Elmundo (www.elmundo.es)
Terra (www.terra.es)
Ya (www.ya.com)

Figure 8.12. Spanish SE buscador.terra.es

National German Search Engines

Most popular German national search engines and directories (by **www. alexa.com**):

Spiegel (www.spiegel.de)
T-online (www.t-online.de)
Web.de (www.web.de)

Figure 8.13. German SE www.web.de

National French Search Engines

Most popular French national search engines and directories (by **www. alexa.com**):

Orange (www.orange.fr)
Voila (www.voila.fr)

Figure 8.14. French SE www.orange.fr

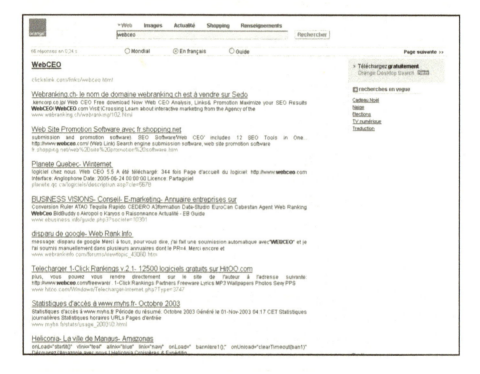

National Chinese Search Engines

About 94 million people in China became Internet users by the end of last year, according to a new survey on internet usage in the world's most populous nation. The number represents a year-on-year growth of 18.2%, the Internet Network Information Centre (CNNIC) found. Among Chinese internet users, men accounted for 60.6% of the total while women made up 39.4%.

More than half of Chinese Internet users were below 25 years of age. Out of the total, 32% were students, 12% professionals and 9% from business and service sectors.

Nearly 67.9% of netizens said they surfed the web mainly at home, while about 40% logged on in offices, Internet cafes and schools.

People use the Internet mostly for email, reading news and searching for information. Nearly nine out of ten users said email service was the most important function of the internet and about 65 per cent of them felt obtaining news was the second most important benefit.

The survey also found that a large number of Internet users rely on it to gain knowledge. About 6.3% said they use the internet as an educational tool.

However, the number of people using e-banking services did not increase much because of security concerns in cyberspace. Only 5% of respondents said they used cyber bank services in their daily lives. (For more information see Chapter 3 Appendix: Search Engines around the World.)

Most popular Chinese national search engines and directories (by **www.alexa.com**):

Baidu (www.baidu.com)
Sina (www.sina.com)
Sohu (www.sohu.com)

Figure 8.15. Chinese SE www.baidu.com

National Japanese Search Engines

Most popular Japanese national search engines and directories (by **www. alexa.com**):

Rakuten (**www.rakuten.co.jp**)
Biglobe (**www.biglobe.ne.jp**)
Goo (**www.goo.ne.jp**)

Figure 8.16. Japanese SE *www.goo.ne.jp*

National Korean Search Engines

Most popular search engines that Koreans use are Daum, Empas and Naver. All three engines are in Korean and target the Korean public. Daum was the fourth most popular website in the world according to Alexa (subsidiary company of amazon.com, which provides information on the web traffic to sites) at one point. It offers number of web services to web users, including a popular free web-based email, messaging service, forums, shopping, and news. Empas is another very interesting search engine, where the quality of answers to each search is rated from one to five. Everyone is welcome to rate each answer. Naver is also an interactive search engine.

With Naver, people post questions on a bulletin board and the INs (frequent users that have more privileges) may choose to answer the question. These questions may range from general questions to personal questions like how to deal with a relationship. After the question is posted anyone may answer. These answers are then rated by the questioner and the answers are given certain points. When enough points are accumulated a person may become a master.

The Internet is widely used by people of all ages; however, it seems that Internet attracts younger people under fifty. The top Internet addicts are Middle School students with 27.5% and High School students with 23.8% of the population online. This is largely due to the developing gaming industry and gaming addiction in South Korea. Gaming has been a large influence for Korean people and has maintained half of the population interested in the Internet these recent years. Email has always been the primary reason for people to use the Internet; however, there has been a decline in recent years. Shopping has changed drastically since 2001. It used to be the second top reason yet its popularity has declined dramatically each year.

According to a ranking site, KoreanClick.com, the most popular search engine is Naver.com, which is visited by about 26 million people a month. The table below was conducted in June 2005 and shows top ten most popular portal sites in Korea.

Figure 8.17. Top Korean Search Engines

Rank	Search site	Number of users per month	Reach (%)
1	Naver.com	26,589,855	93.6
2	Daum.net	26,198,264	92.2
3	Nate.com	23,466,260	82.6
4	kr.Yahoo.com	21,189,959	74.6
5	Paran.com	15,574,483	54.8
6	Dreamwiz.com	12,932,174	45.5
7	Empas.com	12,699,164	44.7
8	Hanafos.com	10,194,372	35.9
9	Chol.com	10,077,267	35.5
10	MSN.co.kr	9,576,769	33.7

Naver (www.naver.com)
Nate (www.nate.com)
Daum (www.daum.net)

Figure 8.18. Korean SE *www.daum.net*

Chapter 9

Longevity in the Jungle (7 steps)

Websites become outdated and die out with time. Out of the millions of sites that are

born, more compete for the same keywords, the same traffic and time in the spotlight. As we said before, you need to take care of your site on continuous basis, protecting against predators (hackers), developing your family and keeping up with what's going on in the jungle. This chapter offers the final word on long-term survival and happiness in the wilderness of the Internet.

Long-term survival is the goal of any species. This is the most difficult task because the more websites are being created, the more competition there is. In order to survive on the web you need to be consistent in fine-tuning your website. To many, consistency is very difficult. Therefore, I recommend contracting professionals for this purpose, or at least seek their advice on how to advance your site.

Having the right tools always at hand will help you survive. Among various multi-purpose programs for site promotion and maintenance, check out Web CEO; it has free tools for almost any possible web-related task and is constantly updated and developed by the team.

You need to actively support your website and update content on main pages and subsections. When you change your content, you need to check if the links on your site are still legitimate. Your content might change a lot over time, and if you leave the same links as your website changes, they can become outdated and irrelevant. If links on your site are not related to content, search engines can penalize your site and put it on the black list. This will harm your ranking and will take time to fix.

Don't forget to check the links that point outside your site, as the content of other websites you are linking to may change without any notification. There are some software packages that will automatically alert you if web pages you are linking to have been removed or changed.

Also, check whether people are using all the sections of your website. If a section is not used, get rid of it. Unused sections die out like dried-up branches of a tree.

Think of your website as a living organism. You need to feed it with dynamic content and links.

In the grand scheme of things, think of three levels of survival:

- The site
- Family and friends, all links
- Overall search cloud. The topic you show must be interesting to people, so it is successful and people purchase your products and/or services.

It is best to build a detailed plan of how you want your website to develop and follow it. But the world is not perfect, so you at least need to check key indicators to ensure survival. You need to monitor what is going on inside and outside your site. Check for broken links; monitor everything concerning traffic, no matter if the site is dynamic or static. Track where the traffic is coming from, which countries, which search engines, what's the quality and conversion.

Always keep an eye on your competitors. Look at where they are advertising and what they are spending.

Keep track of your keywords and phrases. Make sure that they are up-to-date and relevant.

Update your listings in directories and portals. If a certain listing is not generating expected traffic, try to play around with the copy to see if you can make it stand out.

And yes, if you can follow your plan, you have a much better chance of surviving in the Internet Jungle.

The bottom line of your advertising efforts should be your return on investment (ROI). It is the main indicator of how effective your marketing campaign is. One of our friends told us that we should look at advertising as a machine where you put in one dollar and get out two (or more), meaning that when you spend money and time on advertising, you should get back more than you spent. Otherwise, what is the point? (This is true except for large businesses where advertising is used not only to draw revenue but to build brand awareness as well).

However, you should not be hasty in drawing conclusions from your ROI indicators. Many times your ROI will not be what you expect or want. But you need to give it some time because in the Internet Jungle it takes time to integrate into the whole system and reap results. A tree can grow for years before it blooms. We are not suggesting that you wait for years, but you should use your common sense and expert knowledge to identify when and how you are supposed to benefit from your marketing efforts. Integrating a system that analyses the results of your marketing campaign is essential. ROI is a multidimensional matrix, so you need to keep in mind that changes outside of your control may be responsible for shifts in ROI. The web is dynamic, search engines change, content and keywords change, competitors' positions change, bids change, etc. There are always changes, so you need to reposition your website according to what is happening in order to receive the results you want.

Make the mechanics work for you. For example, there is a considerable arbitrage right now in cost of PPC between English-based and non-English based advertising. So the cost of acquiring clients from overseas markets is substantially less than in the US. This window will close soon, but meanwhile, you can make this work for you. Expand your business internationally at a fraction of the cost. There are many opportunities like this on the web. If you can use arbitrage between various acquisition systems outside and inside, you can minimize the cost of acquisition.

9.1. Domain Names

Domain names play an important part in long-term survival. Apart from influencing your website's ranking, the domain name for your website works like names in the outside world because names have meanings and connotations. When someone names a baby, they usually look for a name that fits the baby's character or desired destiny. Domain names should be picked in the same manner. They should sound catchy and have meaning (spiritual/historic). The name should fit the character of your website. The way the name sounds is important because different sounds are interpreted differently in people's minds. Some phrases end on a high note and others on low. Say your website's name out loud and see if you are getting a positive feeling from it. It is important to create positive energy from the start. Even on the web, good karma is important for long-term success.

9.2 Go Global, Go Local

Multiply your site in languages. We suggest that you use only human translators (as opposed to computers) to optimize important content that converts your visitors into buyers. Remember to use hosting located in different places (with different IP addresses) with the search engines in mind.

Use a local domain extension and domain name for a website written in a foreign language. Don't forget about style and cultural differences in each country.

We recommend that you use each country's most popular web hosting (indexed first). Arrange link exchange to reach high link popularity in a short time.

9.3. Participate in Blogs & Forums

Control your webmaster and watch SEO news and gossip in Internet. One large resource that will provide you with fresh ideas and vital information you need for survival is **www.webmasterworld.com**. It's also a good idea to find blogs and forums related to your business – those are usually friendly, informative and flame-free. We have learned a lot while our staff got involved in problem discussion through online multilingual chats.

9.4. Watch Your Diet

Everything is good in moderation. Traffic is good for your website, but the quality of traffic is as important as large numbers. Traffic from adult sites is not appropriate for a website that sells candy. Think of it as junk food: it fills you up, but it does not have the same benefits as healthy food. The same goes for unrelated links. They bring you traffic, but do not translate into conversion.

We expect programs for text quality analysis (linguistic flow) to appear soon. This is a valuable indicator that shows how robust and healthy your site is.

9.5. Watch Your Competitors

Your competitors are watching you, so you need to watch them. Sometimes companies employ hackers to sabotage your site. Remember that hackers can only use holes and security flaws in your website. As long as you abide by standards, rules and instructions before using any new technique or feature (such as a dynamic programming language), your website won't have holes. Protect yourself against intruders by securing your content. Use encryption where possible. Of course, a website that forces its visitors view its home page through secure protocol looks odd, but protecting sensitive content such as the members' area is OK.

Protect your trademarks. Generally, as your site gets stronger it becomes more prone to attacks.

You can set up honey pots to watch for hacker attacks. In computer terminology, a *honeypot* is a trap set to detect or deflect attempts at unauthorized use of information systems. Generally it consists of a computer, data or a network site that appears to be part of a network but is actually isolated and protected, and which seems to contain information that would be of value to attackers. A honeypot that masquerades as an open proxy is known as a *sugarcane*.

A honeypot is valuable as a surveillance and early-warning tool. While often a computer, a honeypot can take on other forms, such as files or data records, or even unused IP address space. Honeypots should not have production value, and hence should not see any legitimate traffic or activity. Whatever they capture can then be surmised as malicious or unauthorized.

Honeypots can carry risks to a network, and must be handled with care. If they are not properly walled off, an attacker can use them to actually break into a system.

9.6. Exercise Daily

A successful website is optimized continuously. Just like with humans, if you don't use it you lose it. A website needs to condition just like a person needs exercise if he or she wants to stay in shape.

You need to plan for how you want your website to grow in terms of parameters, architecture (where you want traffic and traps), content (static and dynamic), and tools for interaction with the outside world. If you are planning to stay at the top of the online world, your website must be built according to what's going to be the best in the future. This means that you need to develop a schedule of what needs to be done every week, every month, etc. The more stringently you follow the schedule, the better ranking you will enjoy over time.

Keep track of the results that you are getting with your efforts. Look at what kind of links people follow from search results, and within your website. Analyze whether each part of your site is used at all, and if not active, kill it off and develop a more active section. Like trees in the Jungle, let the new branches grow, and let the dry branches fall.

9.7. Relax and be Happy

Internet is a unique business medium where you can operate your business from any remote location. You can be at a beach resort with a good wireless Internet connection and control your web business from there, just as if you were sitting in a high tech office. Therefore, geographic location is irrelevant to the operation of your online business. So relax and be happy because positive people make progress.

Afterword

In the Internet Jungle there are winners and losers. Those who follow rules of numbers usually do well on the Internet. However, only those who grasp that the Internet is more than a cold machine and is a living organism can take on a perspective that leads to true success on the Internet. Many have tried to rise from rags to riches, thinking that the Internet works like magic, but the truth is that on the Internet, just as in any other business environment, building wealth takes time. It is actually even truer for the Internet because the major trend now is to set up businesses that consist of a bunch of streams of small revenue. The days of hitting it big overnight are over, but if you are patient and persistent, the Internet Jungle can become your point of success.

Acknowledgements

Special thanks to our research team, whose help was instrumental in creating this book (especially the multilingual sections).

Team Leader:
Nickolas Hoog, English, VP Universal Engine Group, BA: Business

Audrey Petrose, French, BA: International Business
In Whan Cha, Korean BA: Philosophy
Jalpa Gohil, Hindi, Masters: Communication (emphasis on Advertising)
Mark Vinardell, Spanish, BA: Marketing
Martin Kalpein, German, BA: Sports Marketing
Shyan Weng, Chinese/Taiwanese, Master's: Direct an Interactive Marketing
Yozo Suzuki, Japanese, Masters: Communication
Chun Yin Yu, Cantonese Chinese, Mandarin, BA, Economics
Mee Sun Han, Korean, BA, Economics
Monica Mesalles Cervera, Spanish, BA, Advertising & PR
Reyna Hernandez, Spanish, BA, Marketing & International Business
Sirirat (Dolly) Lalitkuntorn, Thai, MBA, Marketing
Corentin Villemeur, French, Masters, Marketing & Business
Efstratios Boudouridis, Greek, BA, Marketing
Ruba Jraije, Arabic, Masters: Advertising

We have not attempted to cite in the text all the sources consulted in the preparation of this manual because the scope of the book is so wide.

Special Thanks

John Holmes, TSV Group for introduction and mentoring us on Fortune 500 Companies

Bill Hunt, President / CEO, Global Strategies International, Search Effective Team Lead, ibm.com, worldwide leader in online international marketing for recognition on international panel at Search Engine Strategy conference in New York

Beryl J. Wolk, Marketing Mogul, who provided M4 (marketing, media, management, money) identity for a Better World

Bob Kramer, without him this book would never have happened

Howard Sterling, **Laura Fund** for not believing in international marketing, but guiding us through reality

Frank Watson, FXCM, word marketer and smart keyword authors for encouraging us to write a book at the lobster fiesta

Massimo Burgio, **Juno** for giving us inside story on Internet marketing in Europe

Steve Aiello, Senior Counselor, Public Affairs of Hill & Knowlton for introduction to WPP group and couching us through big Gorilla marketing

Yuri Baranov, **Sergey Neskhodovsky** WebCEO specialists, for providing information and technical edition this book, including the Glossary

Mark Victor Hansen, Co-creator of *Chicken Soup for the Soul* for coaching us on how to write and distribute the book

Michael Ruge, author of *Quote a Quote* for combining all marketing gurus in the word in one room for strategic sessions

Martin Wales, The Customer Catcher, for positioning the Internet Jungle book

Matt Bacak, the Powerful Promoter and author of "Powerful Promoting Tips" newsletter for showing PR online navigation through Internet Jungle

Warren Whitlock, Author, Marketing Results Coach, and Book Marketing Expert, for sharing blogging skills in the Internet Jingle

Randy Gilbert, Dr. Proactive Internet Talk radio "The Inside Success Show" for showing us how to make friends in Internet Jungle

Michael Islek, Register.com for navigation and coaching while writing this book

Mark Benda and Robert C. Smith, the Genimation Group, for showing how to recognize "purple cow" in marketing

Appendixes

CD included with this book

To make your Internet surviving easier and your Web experience better, we've supplied each copy of this book with a CD containing some great software: Web CEO.

Web CEO became our choice mainly because it has a free license that allows for usage without time constraints. Just run the setup file, register the software and enjoy. Web CEO 6.5 is a suite of tools that approach daily site promotion, maintenance and analysis tasks from nearly every possible angle. It helps you to research keywords, optimize and submit pages, check your rankings, analyze link popularity and effectively look for link partners, plus manage PPC campaigns and analyze visitor traffic, and then some more.

Web CEO Registration also opens access to a wonderful training course where you can dive deep into details of every step of the Web marketing process, and even earn certification if you wish.

Although a seriously good software, the Free Edition of Web CEO has some functional limitations, which can be removed by purchasing the higher license when you decide to.

Also included are Web CEO Quick Start Guide (PDF), and some demo movies that quickly tune you into working with each tool of Web CEO (SWF). Adobe Acrobat Reader is required to open the Quick Start Guide, and Flash Player is required to view the movies. Both can be either installed from the CD or downloaded from the respective Web sites, but you probably already have them on your computer.

CD Note:

To get a CD, please send your name, email and home address to: *internetjungle@gmail.com* and we will gladly send you one.

Multilingual Internet Usage

Top ten languages used in the WEB, millions

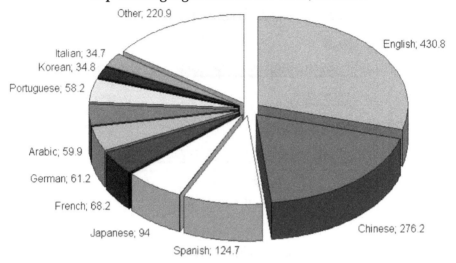

Source: www.internetworldstats.com

Internet users by language, millions

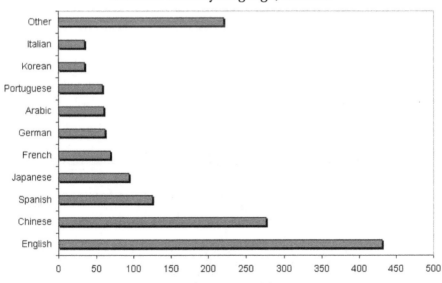

Source: www.internetworldstats.com

World Internet Usage Growth 2000-2008, %

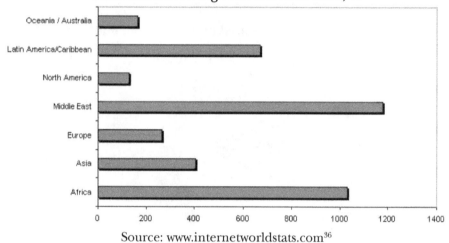

Source: www.internetworldstats.com[36]

**Top 10 countries with the highest number of
Internet DSL broadband subscribers**

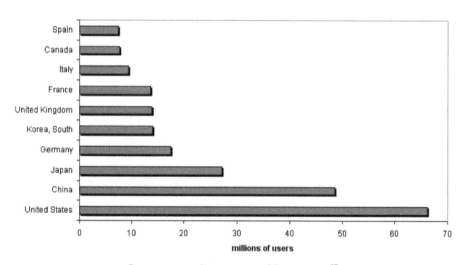

Source: www.internetworldstats.com[37]

---

[36] World Internet usage growth stats were updated in June, 2008
[37] DSL broadband subscribers stats were updated in 2006-2007

Internet population statistics by world regions

World Regions	Population (2008)	Internet Users	Penetration	Usage Growth 2000-2008
Africa	955,206,348	4,514,400	5.3 %	1,031.2 %
Asia	3,776,181,949	114,304,000	15.3 %	406.1 %
Europe	800,401,065	105,096,093	48.1 %	266.0 %
Middle East	197,090,443	3,284,800	21.3 %	1,176.8 %
North America	337,167,248	108,096,800	73.6 %	129.6 %
Latin America/ Caribbean	576,091,673	18,068,919	24.1 %	669.3 %
Oceania/Australia	33,981,562	7,620,480	59.5 %	165.1 %
WORLD TOTAL	6,676,120,288	360,985,492	21.9 %	305.5 %

Source: www.internetworldstats.com[38]

Internet population statistics by the largest countries

Country	Population (2008)	Internet Users	Penetration	Usage Growth 2000-2008
China	1,330,044,605	253,000,000	19.0 %	1,024.4 %
United States	303,824,646	220,141,969	72.5 %	130.9 %
Japan	127,288,419	94,000,000	73.8 %	99.7 %
India	1,147,995,898	60,000,000	5.2 %	1,100.0 %
Germany	82,369,548	52,533,914	63.8 %	118.9 %

Source: www.internetworldstats.com[39]

---

[38] Internet usage and world population statistics were updated in June, 2008
[39] Internet population statistics by the largest countries were updated in June, 2006

Metasearch Tools

Clusty
www.clusty.com
Clusty, from Vivisimo, presents both standard web search results and
Vivisimo's dynamic clusters that automatically categorize results. Clusty
allows you to use Vivisimo's dynamic clustering technology on ten different
types of web content including material from the web, image, weblog and
shopping databases. You can access each type of search by simply clicking
a tab directly above the search box.

CurryGuide
web.curryguide.com
Meta search engine for the US and several European countries, as well as
in various subject areas. Has ability to save your results for easy rerunning
at a future point.

Excite
www.excite.com
Formerly a crawl-based search engine, Excite was acquired by InfoSpace
in 2002 and uses the same underlying technology as the other InfoSpace
Meta search engines, but maintains its own portal features.

Fazzle
www.fazzle.com
Fazzle offers a highly flexible and customizable interface to a wide variety
of information sources, ranging from general web results to specialized
search resources in a number of subject specific categories. Formerly
called SearchOnline.

IceRocket
www.icerocket.com
Meta search engine with thumbnail displays. The Quick View display,
similar to what WiseNut has long offered, is cool. The service queries
WiseNut, Yahoo!, Teoma and then somewhat repetitively also includes
Yahoo!-powered MSN, AltaVista and AllTheWeb. Disclosure of search
sources within the actual search results is not done, sadly. Makes it hard
to know exactly where the results are coming from.

Info.com
www.info.com
Info.com provides results from 14 search engines and pay-per-click directories, including Google, Ask Jeeves, Yahoo!, Kanoodle, LookSmart, About, Overture and Open Directory. Also offers shopping, news, eBay, audio and video search, as well as a number of other interesting features.

InfoGrid
www.infogrid.com
In a compact format, InfoGrid provides direct links to major search sites and topical web sites in different categories. Meta search and news searching also offered.

Ixquick
www.ixquick.com
Meta search engine that ranks results based on the number of "top 10" rankings a site receives from the various search engines.

Izito
www.izito.com
iZito is a meta search engine with a clever feature. Click on any listing you are interested in using the P icon next to the listing title. That "parks" the listing into your to do list. Click on the P tab, and you can see all the pages you've culled. It's an easy, handy way to make a custom result set. Also interesting is the ability to show listings in up to three columns across the screen, letting you see more results at once.

Jux2
www.jux2.com
This search result comparison tool is cool. It allows you to search two major search engines at the same time, see results that are found on both first, followed by results found on only one of them next. The small overlap visual tool displayed is great. I used to make examples like this to explain search engine overlap and why one search engine may not cover everything. Now I have an easy dynamic way to do this. The stats link at the bottom of the home page provides more visuals.

Meceoo

www.meceoo.com

Meta search with the ability to create an "exclusion list" to block pages from particular web sites being included. For example, want to Meta search only against .org sites?

MetaCrawler

www.metacrawler.com

One of the oldest Meta search services, MetaCrawler began in July 1995 at the University of Washington. MetaCrawler was purchased by InfoSpace, an online content provider, in Feb. 97.

MetaEureka

www.metaeureka.com

Search against several major search engines and paid listings services. Offers a nice option to see Alexa info about pages that are listed.

Query Server

www.queryserver.com/web.htm

Search against major web-wide search engines, as well as major news, health, money and government search services.

Turbo10

turbo10.com

Turbo10 is a Meta search engine accesses both traditional web search engines and some invisible web databases, with a very speedy interface.

Search.com

www.search.com

Search.com is a Meta search engine operated by CNET. It offers both web-wide search and a wide variety of specialty search options. Search. com absorbed SavvySearch in October 1999. SavvySearch was one of the older metasearch services, around since May 1995 and formerly based at Colorado State University.

Ujiko

www.ujiko.com

From the makers of visual Meta search tool KartOO, this is a really slick service to try. Do your search, and scroll through the list. See something bad? Click the trash can icon, and the listing goes away. It's a great way to prune your results – it would be even better if everything trashed brought up something new. That would be a help for those who simply refuse to go past the first page of results.

See something you like? Click the heart icon and you can rate the listing. This information is memorized, to help ensure the sites you choose to better in future searches. Unlike KartOO, Ujiko uses results from only one search engine: Yahoo! It also offers many more features I haven't even yet explored.

WebCrawler
www.webcrawler.com
Formerly a crawl-based search engine owned by Excite, Webcrawler was acquired by InfoSpace in 2002 and uses the same underlying technology as the other InfoSpace Meta search engines, but offers a fast, clean, ad-free interface.

ZapMeta
www.zapmeta.com
Provides a variety of ways to sort the results retrieved, plus provides interesting visualization tools and other features.

Family Friendly Search
www.familyfriendlysearch.com
Meta search service that queries major kid-friendly search engines.

GoFish
www.gofish.com
Meta search service for licensed and commercially available digital media downloads including music, movies, music videos, ringtones, mobile games and PC games, searching over 12 million media files.

Searchy.co.uk
www.searchy.co.uk
Searches 15 U.K. engines. The advanced search form allows you to change the order in which results are presented, either by speed or manually to suit your own preferences.

All-In-One Search Pages

Unlike Metacrawlers, all-in-one search pages do not send your query to many search engines at the same time. Instead, they generally list a wide-variety of search engines and allow you to search at your choice without having to go directly to that search engine.

One Page MultiSearch Engines
www.bjorgul.com
Clean interface lets you query major services from one page.

Proteus
www.thrall.org/proteus.html
Lets you easily send your search to one of several search engines. It also has links to search engine help pages.

Search engine comparison by feature

Features	Google	Yahoo!	Ask	Live Search
Boolean	-, OR	AND, OR, NOT,	-, OR	AND, OR, NOT,
Default	and	and	and	and
Proximity	Phrase	Phrase	Phrase	Phrase
Truncation	No (stems)	No	No	No
Fields	intitle, inurl, link, site, more	intitle, inurl, link, site, more	intitle, inurl, site	intitle, site, loc, url
Limits	Language, filetype, date, domain	Language, file type, date, domain	Language, site, date	Language, site
Stop	Few, + searches	No	Yes, + searches	Varies, + searches
Sorting	Relevance, site	Relevance, site	Relevance, metasites	Relevance,site, sliders

Source: www.searchengineshowdown.com/features/byfeature.shtml

Software comparison chart

	Web CEO	WebPosition Gold	AddWeb	IBP (Axandra)
	webceo.com	webposition.com	cyberspacehq.com	axandra.com
General	Unlimited use	30-day trial	30-day trial	30-day trial
Optimization advice	Yes (Optimization Tool)	Yes (Page Critic)	Yes (Page Advisor)	Yes (Top 10 Optimizer)
HTML page builder	No	Yes	Yes	No
HTML page editor	Yes	No (No separate plugin; some functions are realized in Meta Manager, available as a Platinum upgrade service)	Yes (integrated in Page Builder)	No
SE submission	Yes (Submission Tool)	Yes (Submitter)	Yes (Submission)	Yes (SE Submitter)
SE ranking check	Yes (Ranking Checker)	Yes (Reporter)	Yes (Rank Check)	Yes (Search Engine Ranking Checker)
Link popularity analysis	Yes	No	No	No
Link exchange plugin	Yes	No	Yes	Yes
FTP Uploader	Yes (Built-in FTP client)	Yes (Built-in FTP client)	Yes (Built-in FTP client)	No
Site error scan	Yes (Site Auditor)	No special plugin; separate function (Link Defender) available for broken links check—only in the Platinum upgrade	No	No
	Web CEO	WebPosition Gold	AddWeb	IBP (Axandra)

Uptime monitoring	Yes (Monitoring)	No	No	No
Traffic analysis	Yes (Own: HitLens tool)	Yes (WebTrends account)	Yes (SiteStats Live)	No
Scheduler	Yes	Yes	Yes	No
SE Spider Simulation	Yes	No	No	Yes
Code defender	No	Yes (Compress your HTML so that it becomes difficult—yet possible—to parse and steal for others). Available as Platinum upgrade service only.	No	No

Search engines in Europe

Arcor **www.arcor.de**	Banners, buttons, skyscraper	German	Eschborn, Germany
the fixed-line carrier offers data and voice services, it is the # 2 telecom provider in Germany behind Deutsche Telekom			
Biuscapiqua **www.buscapique.com**	Banners, buttons, skyscraper	Spanish	Peru
(description unavailable in English)			
Brujula **www.brujula.net**	**http://www. brujula.net/ english/acerca/**	Spanish, English, French, Italian, Portuguese	Argentina
including web directory, chat, games, news, VoIP, free e-mail, music, etc.			
Cipotes **www.cipotes.net**	Banners, buttons, skyscraper	English, Spanish	Hicksville NY, USA
telephone communications, internet service providers			
CyFind.de **www.at-web.de**	Pay Per Click	English, German	Berlin, Germany
Cyfind.de is the first pay-by-click search machine. It understands itself as advertising platform and search machine.			
eSpotting **www.miva.com**	**http://www.miva. com/us/content/ advertiser/ paypercall.asp**	English, Spanish, German, French, Italian, Swedish	Fort Myers FL, USA
eSpotting media charged advertisers a fee for the targeted search result placement, the company was acquired by findwhat .com (now MIVA) to create an international group in the paid listing sector of internet advertising.			
GoDado **www.godado.com**	**http://godado. com/promote_a_ site-bis_uk.html**	English, Italian, French, German, Spanish	Seregno, Italy
Established in 1999, GoDado is the innovative search engine developed in Italy that guarantees visibility of web offers. Based on pay per click, the GoDado instrument also guarantees quality of its search engine.			
HispanicBusiness **www.hispanicbusiness. com**	http://www. hispanicbusiness. com/advertise/	English	Santa Barbara CA, USA
For nearly a quarter century, Hispanic Business has given a voice to the Hispanic community through integrated channels of print, online and events			
HispanicOnline **www.hispaniconline.com**	http://www. hispaniconline. com/Advertise/	English	Miami FL, USA

HispanicOnline is a Latino web pioneer, which owns hispanic magazine including trends magazines. Offers more news, resources and entertainment options relevant to Latinos.			
KataWeb **www.kataweb.it**	Banners, buttons, skyscraper	Italian	Rome, Italy
KataWeb is a service of consultation online, finance, incluidng e-mail, forums, movies, music, blogs, etc.			
Kompass **www.kompass.com**	http://www.kompass.com/kinl/index.php	English	around the world
worldwide business directory			
LatinWorld **www.latinworld.com**	Banners, buttons, skyscrapers	English, Spanish	Manhattan NY, USA
LatinWorld is building a community of information and resource and directory of internet resources in Latin America and the Caribbean. An objective is to serve as a communication platform for Latin Americans and people interested in Latin American culture.			
Libero **www.libero.it**	Banners, buttons, skyscraper	Italian	Italy
MexicoWeb **www.mexicoweb.com.mx**	Banners, buttons, skyscraper	Spanish	Pedregal, Mexico
Mexico web was born in Nov 1995, mainly with the great idea to create a directory of web pages only for Mexico			
Quepasa **www.quepasa.com**	Banners, buttons, skyscraper	English, Spanish	Phoenix AZ, USA
a portal offering a search engine, news links, email, chat rooms, text translation, online radio, and e-commerce services, all in Spanish			
Rambler **www.rambler.ru**	Banners, buttons, skyscraper	Russian	Moscow, Russia
Rambler Media provides Russian language services in three complementary and integrated business areas: internet services, mobile value added services (MVAS) and television broadcasting			
Splut **www.splut.com**	http://www.splut.com/advertise.htm	English	UK
banner free search directory for the UK web community			
StarMedia **www.starmedia.com**	Banners, buttons, skyscraper	English, Spanish	Miami FL, USA
StarMedia web portal evolved for regional sites; it raised more than $90 million in venture capital in 1998			
Terra **www.terra.es**	Banners, buttons, skyscraper	Spanish	Miami FL, USA
a leading internet services and online content provider targeting Spanish-speaking customers in Spain and Latin America			

Tiscali www.tiscali.com	English, German, Czech, Spanish		Sardinia, Italy
Tiscali has become one of the continent's top ISPs, along with Deutsche Telekom's T-online and France Telecom's Wanadoo.			
Univision www.univision.com	contact: sales@correo. univision.com	English, Spanish	Los Angeles CA, USA
the leading Spanish-language media company in the United States			
Voila www.voila.fr	Pay Per Click	French	Paris, France
includes shopping, travel, bidding, mobiles, etc.			
Xolo www.xolo.com.ni	Banners, buttons, skyscrapers	Spanish	Managua, Nicaragua
includes email, mobile, gambling, etc.			
Yandex www.yandex.ru	http://advertising. yandex.ru/	Russian	Moscow, Russia
Yandex is the largest portal in the Russian Internet today, which offers its users key internet services. According to research studies conducted by Gallup Media, FOM and Comcon, Yandex is the largest resource in Russian Internet, based on the audience size and internet penetration.			

Search engines in Asia

Company name / Website	Type of Ad	Languages supported	Targeted Region
cnforex.com **www.cnforex.com**	Banners, buttons, skyscrapers	Chinese	China
Hexun.com **www.hexun.com**	Banners, buttons, skyscrapers	Chinese	China
Sina.com **www.sina.com**	Banners, buttons, skyscrapers	Chinese/English	China/ Taiwan/ HongKong
Chinagate.com **www.chinagate.com**	Forum, homepage banners	Chinese	Chinese communities
Baidu **www.baidu.com**	Pay Per Click	Chinese	China
Sohu **www.sohu.com**	Banners, buttons, skyscrapers	Chinese/English	China
Netease **www.163.com**	Banners, buttons, skyscrapers	Chinese	China
3721 **www.3721.com**	Banners, buttons, skyscrapers	Chinese	China
Tom **www.tom.com**	Banners, buttons, skyscrapers	Chinese	China
China.com **www.china.com**	Banners, buttons, skyscrapers	Chinese/English	China
Accoona **www.accoona.com**	Banners, buttons, skyscrapers	Chinese/English	English/ Chinese speaking countries
ChinaVista **www.chinavista.com**	Banners, buttons, skyscrapers	Chinese/English	China
Nihao **www.nihao.com**	Banners, buttons, skyscrapers	Chinese/English	Chinese community in Australia
ChinaPages **www.chinapages.com**	Banners, buttons, skyscrapers	Chinese/English	China
Yam **www.yam.com**	Banners, buttons, skyscrapers	Chinese	China
China-Channel **www.china-channel.com**	Banners, buttons, skyscrapers	Chinese/English	English/ Chinese speaking countries
Yehey **www.yehey.com**	Banners, buttons, skyscrapers	English	The Philippines

Odn www.odn.ne.jp	Banners, buttons, skyscrapers	Japanese	Japan
Biglobe www.biglobe.ne.jp	Banners, buttons, skyscrapers	Japanese	Japan
Goo www.goo.ne.jp	Banners, buttons, skyscrapers	Japanese	Japan
Setagayafxclub www.setagayafxclub.com	Banners	Japanese	Japan
Kawase www.e-kawase.com	Banners	Japanese	Japan
Zubaken www.zubaken.net	Banners, buttons, skyscrapers	Japanese	Japan
Jlisting www.jlisting.jp	Banners, buttons, skyscrapers	Japanese	Japan
Forexchannel.net www.forexchannel.net	Banners	Japanese	Japan
Forexwatcher www.forexwatcher.com	Banners	Japanese	Japan
Chol (Cholian) www.chol.com	Banners, buttons, skyscrapers	Korean	Korea
Naver www.naver.com	Banners, buttons, skyscrapers	Korean	Korea
Ready www.ready.co.kr	Banners, buttons, skyscrapers	Korean	Korea
Daum www.daum.net	Banners, buttons, skyscrapers	Korean	Korea
Korea.com www.korea.com	Banners, buttons, skyscrapers	Korean	Korea
Heeya www.heeya.com	Banners, buttons, skyscrapers	Korean	Korea
Gowww http://gowww.net	Banners, buttons, skyscrapers	Korean	Korea
Empass www.empas.com	Banners, buttons, skyscrapers	Korean	Korea

Glossary

ABM Automated Bid Manager

AdWords uses keywords to precisely target the delivery of advertisements to people seeking out information about a particular product or service. Advertisers choose which keywords they want their ads associated with, then their ads appear alongside Google search results and on web pages with information related to that keyword. AdWords appear as clean, simple text and are clearly identified as promotional, thereby respecting and enhancing web users' efforts to find useful information. Google AdWords offers cost-per-click (CPC) pricing, so advertisers only pay when an ad is clicked on. Advertisers can take advantage of an extremely broad distribution network, as ads can appear alongside Google.com search results, with search results on Google's partner sites (AOL, Ask Jeeves, and others), and on targeted content pages on leading websites. Advertisers can choose the level of support and spending as is appropriate for their business. AdWords is available on a self-service basis, in which advertisers control the details of their campaign – creative, keyword choices and daily budget – via online tools and with email support. Advertisers with more extensive campaigns and budgets can receive strategic services, which include an account team of experienced professionals that will help them set up, manage, and optimize their campaigns. For more information about Google search advertising opportunities, visit www.google.com/ads.

Animated ad contains movement, often an interactive Java applet or Shockwave or GIF89a file.

API Application Programming Interface

ASCII American Standard Code for Information Interchange

Banner ad is a graphic image, usually a GIF or JPEG, that can be placed anywhere on a web page, most frequently centered across the top. The tile ad is a smaller counterpart, typically grouped with other tile ads along a side margin. The standard banner ad is 468 x 60 pixels; the most common size for tile ads is 125 x 125 pixels.

Beyond-the-banner is the name for any advertisement that is not a banner, such as an interstitial or a pop-up ad.

Blacklisted, in SEO terms, refers to being banned from submitting to a particular search engine.

Blind Traffic low quality traffic that is usually generated by misleading advertising, spam, and traffic from any market segment.

Blog = weB LOG, basically a journal that is available on the web. The activity of updating a blog is "blogging" and someone who keeps a blog is a "blogger." Blogs are typically updated daily using software that allows people with little or no technical background to update and maintain the blog. Postings on a blog are almost always arranged in chronological order with the most recent additions featured most prominently. It is common for blogs to be available as RSS feeds.

Blogosphere refers to the current state of all information available on blogs and/or the sub-culture of those who create and use blogs.

Boolean search a search formed by joining simple terms with AND, OR and NOT for the purpose of limiting or qualifying the search. If you search information on salmon fishing in Alaska, and your search also brings back information on trout fishing and diving in Alaska, the Boolean search "salmon AND fishing AND Alaska NOT diving" can narrow your search focus.

Broken Link is a link that no longer takes the user to the destination page when it is clicked on. This is usually the result of the destination page having been renamed or deleted from the server. A broken link is also referred to as a Dead Link.

Button is a clickable graphic that takes the user to another page or executes a program, such as a software demo or a video player.

Call to action refers to ad copy that encourages users to take a defined action. Examples range from "Click here" or "Buy now" to "Enter now to win a free trip to Hawaii" or "Click to download a free sheet of white paper."

Call-to-action link is otherwise known as a hyperlink. Call-to-action links in Internet marketing campaigns guide the reader to a new action step. Call-to-action hyperlinks could lead a prospect to a new Web page, an email form, a text section within a page or a shopping cart. Correctly written, call-to-action links increase micro-conversion rates and can affect keyphrase relevancy.

Click-down ad is an ad that allows the user to stay on the same web page while viewing requested advertising content. Click-downs display another file on the user's screen, normally below or above the initial ad. Click withins allow the user to drill down for more information within the ad.

Click popularity measures the relevence of search results by monitoring user behavior from the search results. If a user clicks on a result and returns to the SERPs within a short period, the site is viewed as less relevant and is thus downgraded in the rankings. Similarly, if click-through rates on the first page of results are low and users have to click through to the second or third page to find relevant results, this is taken into consideration when re-ordering results. Click popularity algorithms are one of the most effective ways of presenting relevant search results. However, they are vulnerable to manipulation by click-bots which attempt to artificially boost click-through rates. A pioneer in click popularity was Direct Hit. Elements of the Direct Hit algorithm are still used by Ask Jeeves.

Clickthrough the process of clicking on a link in a search engine output page to visit an indexed site. This is an important link in the process of receiving visitors to a site via search engines. Good ranking may be useless if visitors do not click on the link which leads to the indexed site. The secret here is to provide a good descriptive title and an accurate and interesting description.

Clickthrough rate (CTR) es the number of clickthroughs divided by the number of impressions, multiplied by 100 and expressed as a percentage. For example, your CTR is one percent if 100 people are shown your ad and one person clicks through to your site. CTRs typically range from 0.5 percent for banner ads to 3.0 percent for text links. Also known as ad impression ratio or yield.

Cloaking is the art of delivering different content to different users based on their IP address or user-agent string. There are a few different uses for cloaking such as delivering content to people from different countries. It is also used to deliver different search engine optimised content to the search engines and then different content to the users. This is deemed to be unethical in the eyes of search engines as people stuff the cloaked pages with links and repeat keywords in order to rank highly, while giving the users standard-looking pages.

Clustering in search engine search results pages, clustering is limiting each represented website to one or two listings.

Comment Tag an HTML tag that is invisible to end-users, but can be picked up by search engines.

Comment the HTML tags are used to hide text from browsers. Some search engines ignore text between these symbols but others index such text as if the comment tags were not there. Comments are often used to hide javascript code from non-compliant browsers, and sometimes (notably on Excite) to provide invisible keywords to some search engines.

Content integration references advertising woven into editorial content or placed in a special context on the page, typically appearing on portals and large destination sites. Also known as web advertorial or sponsored content.

Content targeting is the ability to run relevant ads on content websites, rather than on search results pages. The first generation of content targeting (also known as contextual advertising) required manual insertion of relevant ads on informational sites related to the search query. Now content targeted advertising can also be dynamic: the ad system sees you are viewing a page about travel (the "content"), by having examined words on the page and other factors, and therefore delivers up an ad related to travel (the "context"). Also known as content-targeted advertising.

Conversion is a defined reaction in response to your ad's call to action. A conversion may be a sale, or it could be a registration, download, or entry into your lead database, depending on the goal of your campaign.

Conversion rate refers to the number of visitors who respond to your ad's call to action divided by the number of impressions, multiplied by 100 and expressed as a percentage. For example, your conversion rate is one percent if 100 people are shown your ad, the five people click through to your site and the one person makes a purchase. Conversion rates are distinct measurements that determine how many of your prospects take your preferred action step. Typically, micro-conversions (for instance, reading different pages on your site, or signing up for a newsletter) lead to your main conversion step (making a purchase, or contacting you for more information).

Cookie refers to a piece of information sent by a Web Server to a Web Browser that the Browser software is expected to save and send back to the server whenever the browser makes additional requests from the server. Depending on the type of Cookie used and the Browsers' settings, the Browser may accept or not accept the Cookie, and may save the Cookie for either a short time or a long time. Cookies might contain information such as login or registration information, online "shopping cart" information, user preferences, etc. When a Server receives a request from a Browser that includes a Cookie, the Server is able to use the information stored in the Cookie. For example, the server might customize what is sent back to the user, or keep a log of particular users' requests. Cookies are usually set to expire after a predetermined amount of time and are usually saved in memory until the browser software is closed down, at which time they may be saved to disk if their "expire time" has not been reached. Cookies do not read your hard drive and send your life story to the CIA, but they can be used to gather more information about a user than would be possible without them.

Counter program that tracks the number of impressions to a webpage.

Cost-per-action CPA pricing based on the number of actions in response to your ad. An action may be defined as a sales transaction, a customer acquisition, or simply a click. Also known as cost-per-transaction. CPA may also refer to cost-per-acquisition.

Counter program that tracks the number of impressions to a webpage.

Cost-per-click (CPC) pricing is based on the number of clicks your ad receives. A typical range is 5 cents to $1 per click. Also known as pay-per-click. CPC may also refer to cost-per-customer.

Cost-per-lead (CPL) pricing is based on the number of new leads generated by your ad. For example, you might pay for every visitor that clicks on your ad and successfully completes a form on your site.

Cost-per-order (CPO) pricing is based on the number of orders received as a result of your ad placement. Also known as cost-per-transaction.

Cost-per-sale (CPS) pricing is based on the number of sales transactions your ad generates. Since users may visit your site several times before making a purchase, you can use cookies to track their visits from your landing page to the actual online sale. Also known as cost-per-acquisition or pay-per-sale.

Cost-per-thousand-impressions (CPM) pricing is based on number of impressions served over a period of time. A $50 CPM means you pay $50 for every 1,000 times your ad appears. ("M" is the Roman numeral for 1,000.) Also known as pay-per-impression.

CPM Cost per 1,000 impressions.

Crawler is another name for a search engine spider, a robotic program that visits and downloads web pages and stores them to be inspected by the search engines later.

Crawling the web is job of the search engine crawler. It will follow a set list of pre-defined links that are deemed worthwhile to follow.

Cross-linking is the process by which an owner of one or more domains can interlink them together in order to inflate their link popularity. The search engines are not to keen on this type of linking as it is normally used by people to increase their rankings. Cross-linking is the practice over-using links between a network of sites to artificially inflate link popularity and thus rankings. Google has updated its algorithm to identify clusters of sites which are strongly linked together but not well linked to the rest of the web, and applies a penalty to these sites. Many innocent sites have been affected by this cross-linking penalty as it is a common practice to link to a corporate headquarters from every page of a subsidiary site.

CSS (Cascading Style Sheet) is a standard for specifying the appearance of text and other elements. CSS was developed for use with HTML in Web pages but is also used in other situations, notably in applications built using XPFE. CSS is typically used to provide a single "library" of styles that are used over and over throughout a large number of related documents, as in a website. A CSS file might specify that all numbered lists are to appear in italics. By changing that single specification the look of a large number of documents can be easily changed.

CTR Click Through Ratio.

Dead Link a link to a page that does not exist, probably because the page no longer exists, the page has moved, or the server is down. Automated programs can be used to check your website to ensure such dead links do not exist. A dead link leads to a '404 error page'.

Density refers to number of keywords on a page compared to the total number of words—expressed as a percent.

Description is explanatory text which concisely gives details on the purpose of a page. A Meta tag exists for this, and is used by some search engines when displaying the page as a result in SERPs.

DHTML Dynamic Hypertext Markup Language

Directory is a compilation of websites reviewed and organized by human editors into useful categories and topics, similar to the organization of the Yellow Pages. Examples of directories are Yahoo!, About.com and the Open Directory Project. Directories can be a web page or an entire website dedicated to listing Internet pages. Directories use human editors to review and categorize sites for acceptance and are compiled manually by user submission. Sites such as UKwizz have their own directories that accept websites submitted from the general public. The biggest directory is the Open Directory Project, which has members of the public editing the categories. Many other sites now use a Yahoo!-like directory including major portal sites. Submission to directories is important because they provide a long-term link to your site from a relevant page—it will increase your link popularity, and, as a minor advantage—you can expect some traffic from them. Each directory listing contains short, descriptive information about the site. Strong directory listings are an excellent way your company can increase its link popularity and its Google PageRank. However, a poorly written listing that is submitted to Yahoo! (and subsequently edited or run with ineffective writing or keyword research) can negatively influence a search marketing campaign.

DMOZ Directory MOZilla

DNS is a distributed Internet directory service. DNS is used to translate between domain names and IP addresses, and to control Internet email delivery. DNS is a globally distributed system consisting of thousands of servers sharing information.

Domain is a sub-set of internet addresses. Domains are hierarchical, and lower-level domains often refer to particular web sites within a top-level domain. The most significant part of the address comes at the end. Typical top-level domains are .com, .edu, .gov, .org (which sub-divide addresses into areas of use). There are also various geographic top-level domains (e.g. .ru, .ca, .fr, .ua etc.) referring to particular countries. The relevance of search engine terminology is that websites which have their own domain name (e.g. http://www.webceo.com) will often achieve better positioning than websites which exist as a sub-directory of another organization's domain

Domain Name is the unique name that identifies an Internet site. Domain Names always have two or more parts, separated by dots. The part on the left is the most specific, and the part on the right is the most general. A given machine may have more than one Domain Name but a given Domain Name points to only one machine. Usually, all of the machines on a given Network will have the same thing as the right-hand portion of their Domain Names. It is also possible for a Domain Name to exist but not be connected to an actual machine. This is often done so that a group or business can have an Internet email address without having to establish a real Internet site. In these cases, some real Internet machines must handle the mail on behalf of the listed Domain Name.

Doorway page is specifically designed for the search engines to rank well. One would be designed for Google and one for Yahoo! The pages would be differently optimized to rank well on both. When a normal user visits the page it will either detect their IP address, and then redirect them to the correct page (cloaking) or it will have a large link for them click through to the full site. Either way it is not a great practice to use this type of tactic.

Dynamic content is information on web pages which changes or is changed automatically, e.g. based on database content or user information. Sometimes it's possible to spot that this technique is being used, e.g. if the URL ends with .asp, .cfm, .cgi or .shtml. It is possible to serve dynamic content using standard (normally static) .htm or .html type pages, though. Search engines will currently index dynamic content in a similar fashion to static content, although they will not usually index URLs which contain the "?" character.

Dynamic IP address changes every time your PC or Mac logs onto the Internet. People who blog spam would either use an Internet Service Provider who gave out dynamic IP addresses or would connect to a proxy server which hides their IP address while online.

Exclusive is used to describe a contract that allows advertisers to purchase all inventory on a given page or for chosen keywords.

Expandable banner is an ad that can expand to as large as 468 x 240 pixels after a user clicks on it or after a user moves the cursor over the banner.

External and internal links From a Web site's point of view, outbound links on a specific page can be internal and external. Internal links are pointing to other pages on your site. External links lead to other sites. Having many internal links is a good thing for increasing your site's link popularity, because search engines evaluate all links to a specific Web page, though not all links are considered equal.

Fake Copy Listings Sometimes a malicious company will steal a web page or the entire contents of a web site, re-publish at a different URL and register with one or more search engines. This can cause a loss of traffic from the original site if the search engines position the copy higher in the listings. If you find that someone has stolen your site in this way, write to the company concerned and ask them to remove the stolen content. Also contact the hosting service used by the company, any company that benefits from the theft and any search engine(s) concerned. If the thieves refuse to remove the material or ignore you, obtain legal advice. It is also well worth having printed evidence to support your claim that your copy of the material was there first, and that you have the copyright! See also Mirror Sites.

Filter is used to remove web pages that use spam to promote their pages. A filter is a software application that is used on web pages that have been crawled by the spiders to filter the spam out such as hidden text and hidden links. Filter is a software routine that examines web pages during a robot's crawl looking for search engine spam. If the filter detects the use of spam on the page, a ranking penalty is assessed. Common filters look for hidden text, links to bad neighborhoods, and many other SEO techniques that the search engine doesn't like.

Filter Words are Stop Words such as "is", "am", "were", "was", "the", "for", "do", that search engines deem irrelevant for indexing purposes.

Floating ads appear within the main browser window on top of the page's normal content, appearing to "float" over the top of the page.

Frames describe an HTML technique which allows a webmaster to display two or more separate web pages within a single browser screen. Sites using frames are quite problematic for search engines to crawl and may not be indexed properly. Search engines often will only index pages linked within the <NOFRAMES> tag. If your site utilizes frames, it is highly recommended that you build a site map for your website, and link to it from within your <NOFRAMES> tag.

Frequency is the number of times an ad is delivered to the same browser in a single session or time period. A site can use cookies to track frequency.

Frequent visitors have different visit frequency patterns. Note that unique visitors are reported under 'Frequent visitors'—they are just grouped by their visit frequency patterns.

FTP File Transfer Protocol

Gateway Page is a web page submitted to a search engine (spyder) to give the relevance-algorithm of that particular spyder the data it needs, in the format that it needs it, in order to place a site at the proper level of relevance for the topic(s) in question. (This determination of topical relevance is called "placement.") A gateway page may present information to the spyder, but obscure it from a casual human viewer. The gateway page exists so as to allow a website to present one face to the spyder, and another to human viewers. There are several reasons why one might want to do this. One: the author may not want to publicly disclose placement tactics. Another could be that the format that may be easiest for a given spyder to understand may not be the format that the author wishes to present to his viewers for aesthetics. Still another may be that the format that is best for one spyder may differ from that which is best for another. By using gateway pages, you can present your site to each spyder in the way which is known or thought to be best for that particular spyder. Also known as bridge pages, doorway pages, entry pages, portals or portal pages.

Geo-targeting refers to the distribution of ads to a particular geographical area. For example, you can use a place name in your keyword, such as "London museum" or "Kiev symphony orchestra" Some search engines allow you to target specific countries – and languages – without using keyword relevance.

Google Bombing a method of getting a large number of backlinks targeting one keyword phrase in the link text so that a web page will come up for that keyword. For example: search "miserable failure" in Google.

Google bot is the name given to the Google spider that crawls the web looking for webpages. It can be recognised by the user-agent string which has Goolgebot in it.

Google is the leading search engine on the internet today with approximately 80% of all search traffic. When people speak of search engine optimization (SEO), they're often referring specifically on ranking with Google.

Google Toolbar a downloadable toolbar for Internet Explorer that allows a user to do a Google search without visiting the Google website. The toolbar also displays the Google PageRank (PR) of the page currently displayed in the browser. The latest version also includes a very good popup-blocker. The Google Toolbar is a must have for every serious webmaster. The Google Toolbar can be downloaded here: http://toolbar.google.com.

GOOGOL is the number 1 followed by 100 zeros.

Hidden links are involved in unethical practice in which search engine optimizers may place links on a site and then hide them by making them the same color as the background, or hiding them behind a CSS div.

Hidden text, much like hidden links, is the art of hiding text on the webpage to influence search engine rankings. They can be hidden by making the text the same color as the webpage or using a CSS div and hiding the text in there.

Hit is a single request from a browser for a single item from a Web server. This can be any file — image, download, animation, audio, video, PDF,

Word, Excel, RTF document, etc. To load a single Web page consisting of an html file, eight graphics, one CSS file and two external JavaScripts, the server will get twelve hits. In log file analyzers, 'hits' are often used as a measure of server activity. The term is commonly misused. Many people think of a hit as a visit to one of their web pages. This is incorrect. A hit takes place every time a file is accessed on your website. For example, let's say your friend's home page has a logo gif and 12 pictures on it. Every time a visitor loads that page, 14 hits are recorded: one for the logo gif, 12 for the pictures, and one for the page itself. So don't be all that impressed if he boasts that his site receives 1000 hits a day. In our example, those 1000 hits could have been generated by as few as 72 visitors to the site. The only meaningful way to evaluate the traffic flow of a site is to consider the average daily or monthly number of unique visitors and page views a site receives.

Home Page or Homepage several meanings. Originally, it refers to the web page that your browser is set to use when it starts up. The more common meaning refers to the main web page for a business, organization, person or simply the main page out of a collection of webpages, e.g. "Check out so-and-so's new Home Page."

Host ping is a service that checks your server's IP address for accessibility. The monitoring center sends an ICMP packet to your server's echo port and listens for a response. When the echoed packet is received from the host server, it is compared with the original packet sent. If the data matches, the host server is considered accessible.

HTM Three letter file extension for Hypertext Markup Language (file.htm)

HTML Hypertext Markup Language (file.html)

HTTP Hypertext Transfer Protocol

HTTPS Hypertext Transfer Protocol Secure

Hyperlink is a blue, underlined word or phrase that, when clicked, takes users to another Web pageor section. Hyperlinks are also known as call-to-action links

IBL (In Bound Link) is any link on another page that points to the subject page. Also called a back link.

IBL (Inbound Link) is a link from another site to your site.

ICANN Internet Corporation for Assigned Names and Numbers

Image Map a set of hyperlinks attached to areas of an image. This may be defined within a web page, or as an external file. If the image map is defined as an external file, search engines may have problems indexing your other pages, unless you duplicate the links as conventional text hyperlinks. If the image map is included within the web page, the search engines should have no problem following the links, although it's good practice to provide text links to aid the visually impaired and those accessing the web with graphics switched off or using text only browsers

Impression is an ad served to a user's browser. Number of impressions determines the cost of online ads in CPM pricing models. Also known as an exposure.

Inbound and Outbound links there are two types of links on a page: inbound (links on other sites to yours) and outbound links (links on your Web page to other sites). "Backward links" is another term for inbound links that came into general use through the Google's "Backward links" option in the "Page Info" menu of the Google toolbar. Inbound links increase your site's link popularity, while the outbound links on your site increase the popularity of the destination page. Experts recommend having many inbound and few outbound links.

Index the front cover to the website in a website's home page . You must get your site's overall theme and content across on this page for both the user and the search engine.

Indexability (spiderability) refers to –a site's capacity to be indexed or recorded by a search engine spider. If a site is not indexable, or if a site has reduced indexability, positioning will suffer.

Indexing is the process by which search engines collect information and include it into their database of search results. The process involves extracting the machine-readable text from web pages, and storing it in a format that can be efficiently searched. Indexing is carried out by search engine spiders.

Internal and External Pages Internal pages are on the Web site that you have scanned. If a page is found in any other domain, it is considered an external page.

Interstitial ad an ad page that appears for a short period of time before the user-requested page is displayed. Also known as a transition ad, splash page, or Flash page.

Inventory is advertising space available for purchase on a website. Based on projections, inventory may be specified as number of impressions or as a share of voice. Also known as ad avail.

IP Address a unique numerical Internet Protocol Address that is assigned to every computer that connects to the internet. IP addresses can be either static or dynamic (changes with every internet connection). Your computer's IP address is what enables it to be "found" on the internet in order to receive email, web pages, etc.

IP Delivery is similar to agent name delivery. This technique presents different content depending on the IP address of the client. It is very difficult to view pages hidden using this technique, because the real page is only visible if your IP address is the same as (for example) a search engine's spider.

IP Internet Protocol

JS Javascript (file.js)

KEI Measuring and comparing the demand for your keyword (Daily World Searches) against the number of Web pages that include it (Competition) is a helpful approach to pick up the best keywords. The resulting ratio, KEI or "Keyword Effectiveness Index" will give an idea of how important a specific keyword is. The formula for KEI is KEI = $(DS^2/C) = (DS/C * DS)$, where DS is the number of daily world searches and C is the competition. The KEI range goes from 0 to over 400: 0-10 = Poor keyword; 10-100 = Good Keyword; 100-400+ = Excellent Keyword. Keywords with the highest KEI combine popularity and less competition. It means that it is more likely that you will get a high ranking, if you use these keywords for optimizations.

Key phrase is a group of keywords which appear in the content of a site page. In order for a search engine to return a page in it list of results, it is vital that the targeted search terms appear as key phrases in the web site copy with the appropriate weighting so that its algorithm will find the page a suitable match. A good SEO will have experience in ensuring the copy of the page is optimised for the targeted search terms while still providing useful and informative copy for the user. "Key phrase" is often (incorrectly) used interchangeably with "search term."

Keyphrase search is for documents containing an exact sentence or phrase specified by a user in a search engine text box.

Keyword Density is the ratio of the keyword frequency as compared to the total words found on a page. Online tools can be used to compare keyword densities for multiple pages. With this knowledge, one can build up a page with a similar density as other high ranking pages.

Keyword Domain Name is the use of keywords as part of the URL to a website. Positioning is improved on some search engines when keywords are reinforced in the URL.

Keyword Frequency denotes how often a keyword appears in a page or in an area of a page. In general, higher the number of times a keyword appears in a page, higher its search engine ranking. However, repeating a keyword too often in a page can lead to that page being penalized for spamming.

Keyword nesting is placing one keyword or keyword phrase inside a broader keyword term.

Keyword is a specific word, or combination of words, entered into a search engine that results in a list of pages related to the keyword. A keyword is the content of a search engine query.

Keyword phrase is a two or more word term that defines a keyword in more detail. Used by searchers to find a product.

Keyword Prominence denotes how close to the start of an area of a page that a keyword appears. In general, having the keyword closer to the start of an area will lead to an improvement in the search engine ranking of a page.

Keyword Purchasing is the buying of search keywords from search engines, usually to control banner ad placement. All the major search engines (except EuroSeek and GoTo) insist that keyword purchasing is only used for banner ad placement, and doesn't influence search results.

Keyword research is the process in SEO of finding the keywords or keyword phrases customers use to find a product or service.

Keywords are words or phrases that search engine users enter into the query boxes, when they look for relevant Web pages. If your Web page has apt keywords, it has every chance to of attracting qualified traffic to your site. The Keyword may be a single word or phrase. The term 'Keyphrase' is often used to define a combination consisting of two or more keywords. As far as SEO is concerned, keywords and keyphrases are no different. Major search engines rank pages based on keywords placement within different Web page areas, such as an HTML title, texts in the Body, anchor names and various other tags. This makes keyword placement an essential part of website optimization for search engines. Keyword optimization focuses on placing the best possible keywords in the areas of a Web page that are considered most important by search engines. Good keywords are ones that are often searched for by search engine users and have little competition.

Landing page is an active web page where Internet users will "land" when they click your online ad. Your landing page doesn't need to be your home page. In fact, ROI usually improves if your landing page directly relates to your ad and immediately presents a conversion opportunity — whether that means signing up for a newsletter, downloading a software demo, or buying a product. Also known as a destination URL or clickthrough URL. Landing pages are pages that users would click through to from a PPC campaign or XML feed. For best results, these pages are highly targeted for the reader and specific to the PPC ad or feed description (for instance, if a PPC ad advertises a coat sale, sending prospects to the company home page would invoke frustrations and decrease conversions). Rewriting landing pages is one of the easiest ways companies can increase their conversion rates.

Link can be text or image that connects to web pages together. There are many terms for links, inbound links, backlinks, external links and internal links.

Link exchange in an Internet marketing campaign is the process of exchanging hyperlinks with a quality site that is somehow related to a company's product or service. For instance, a public relations agency may link to a search engine positioning firm's article on "PR and SEO marketing." The SEO may then include a link on their site listing the public relations company. Good link exchange vendors can increase a company's PageRank and increase the number of targeted visitors. Poor link exchanges (think $99 "link farms" where a company promises to link your site to thousands of others) can actually harm site positioning.

Link farm is a web page created for search engine ranking purposes that consists entirely of a long list of unrelated links. These types of pages are penalized by almost all search engines, including Google. Otherwise known as free for all links pages (FFA).

Link popularity is an important factor in search engine optimization and positioning. Search engines use link popularity as a factor in deciding how important your website is. This was Google's simple but brilliant contribution to web search; popular or relevant pages will tend have more links and should therefore be ranked higher. In addition, link popularity is much more difficult to manipulate artificially than on-page factors, and is thus less open to abuse. Link popularity is calculated firstly by counting the amount of websites that link to yours. However, more links do not necessarily mean better positioning as search engines also measure the quality of these incoming links. If your site enjoys links from other well-linked sites then your link popularity is further boosted. Additionally, some search engines, for example Google, are increasingly attempting to refine their link popularity calculations by paying attention to the theme of a link. Some new search engines, like Teoma, are taking this a step further and only counting links within certain web 'communities' of similar themed websites.

Link Reputation is how the search engine refers to the link by evaluating the link text.

Link strategy is the method used by a particular site owner to increase the number of inbound links to their pages and boost their site's link popularity.

Link text is the visible text contained within an <A></A> or anchor tag that provides instructions or information to the viewer.

Linking is the process of placing a link to another web page (usually on another web site) on one of your own web pages.

Links is a short form of the term "hypertext link". A link can point from one document to another or to any resource in fact. It might be inside or outside the current document. Hyperlinked text is usually highlighted in some way. The default is blue underlined text, but it may vary. If there were no links, you would not be able to get from one Web page to another. Typically, you click on the hyperlink to follow it. Sometimes they are a picture or sometimes an icon. They can also appear as a word, image, icon, or another graphic element which can be activated by the click of a mouse. In the source code of a document, a link is a special set of characters that includes a destination URL.

Log File is a file maintained on a server in which details of all file accesses are stored. Analyzing log files can be a powerful way to find out about a web site's visitors, where they come from and which queries are used to access a site. Log files are generated and maintained by the server and contain all details of any file accesses. This includes data such as file accessed, date and time accessed, referring page, user agent, and more. Analyzing log files can be a powerful way to obtain information about visitors and their behavior on your website. Log files are also used to track search engine referrals, and are a good way to find keywords to target for search engine optimization.

Log File Analyzer The primary purpose of server logs is to provide information on server performance and register errors. However, they turned out to be helpful as sources of visitor information. This info is extracted from the logs and given in a legible format to end-users. The software programs that process log files and interpret server events are called log analyzers. They are installed either on the server side or on a user's PC. In the first case, the end users need to access their site reports through a Web interface, while in the second case they should download server logs to their PCs. In both cases, there will be a lag between the time the log was created and when Web site statistics are reported and viewed.

Manual Submission the process of submitting Websites or Web pages to search engines and directories for inclusion in their databases using specific guidelines unique to each index. When people look for a submission tool, they often think about something that saves them a lot of work. However, there are some important submissions that require some work. Submissions to large directories such as Yahoo! and DMOZ are considered strategic. We recommend that you submit to these and other directories manually. Each directory is unique in its category structure, requirements and title/description length. Read the submission guidelines carefully to learn the best approach to directories. Search engines sometimes prevent automated submissions by including an image that has a special code that must be typed in, together with the site data. Submission to these search engines can only be manual. Some search engines and directories only accept paid submissions or paid options have advantages like prominent position or regular updating of a Web page in the index. There are bid-for-placement auctions like Overture, a pioneer in this area. These are also called pay-per-click search engines. You can only submit to this type of engine manually. You will find the 'best of breed' directories and search engines wanting manual submissions in our 'Manual Submission' section. On the information page, there are some facts about these search engines that help.

META Description Syntax: <META name="Description" content="Web page description"> This Meta tag provides a brief description of a Web page. It is important the description is clear about the purpose of the page. The importance of the Description tag for ranking purposes has decreased significantly over the years, but there are still search engines supporting this tag. They log descriptions of the indexed pages and often display them with the title in their results.

META Keywords Syntax: <META name="Keywords" content="keyword1, keyword2, keyword3"> This Meta tag lists words or phrases about the contents of a Web page. It provides some extra text for crawler-based search engines. However, because of frequent attempts to abuse their system, most search engines ignore this tag. Please note that none of the major crawler-based search engines, except for Inktomi, supports the Keywords Meta tag.

META Robots Syntax: <META name="Robots" content="INDEX,FOLLOW"> The Robots' instructions are normally placed in robots.txt file that is uploaded to the root directory of a domain. However, if a Webmaster does not have access to /robots.txt, then instructions can be placed in a Robots META tag. This tag tells the search engine robot whether a page should be indexed, included its database and its links followed.

Meta Robots Tag is an HTML tag that instructs spiders to either index the page or not. Common uses are all, none, index, noindex, follow and nofollow.

Meta Search is a search of searches. A query is submitted to more than one search engine or directory, and results are reported from all the engines, possibly after removal of duplicates and sorting. Also the Meta search engine of the same name, found at http://www.metasearch.com/

This is a way of searching in which results are taken from various sources and then consolidated into a single SERP.

Meta Search Engine compiles its results from many different search engines and returns them in one combined listing. An up-and-coming Meta search engine is Vivisimo. Other well-known Meta search engines are IxQuick and Dogpile. Many surfers use Meta search engines as a convenient way to collate the best results from many different sources. In fact, many surfers don't even realize they are using Meta search engines. A general trend has developed in the last couple of years, whereby some search engines will combine a number of different sources for their results. For example, Freeserve currently uses Overture and Yahoo! to enhance its listings.

Meta tag is a construct placed in the HTML header of a web page, providing information which is not visible to browsers. The most common Meta tags (and those most relevant to search engines) are KEYWORDS and DESCRIPTION. The KEYWORDS tag allows the author to emphasize the importance of certain words and phrases used within the page. Some search engines will respond to this information—others will ignore it. Don't use quotes around the keywords or keyphrases. The DESCRIPTION tag allows the author to control the text of the summary displayed when the page appears in the results of a search. Again, some search engines will ignore this information. The HTTP-EQUIV Meta tag is used to issue HTTP commands, and is frequently used with the REFRESH tag to refresh page content after a given number of seconds. Gateway pages sometimes use this technique to force browsers to a different page or site. Most search engines are wise to this, and will index the final page and/or reduce the ranking. Infoseek has a strong policy against this technique, and they might penalize your site, or even ban it. Other common Meta tags are GENERATOR (usually advertising the software used to generate the page) and AUTHOR (used to credit the author of the page, and often containing email address, homepage URL and other information).

Metacrawler a Meta search engine found at http://www.metacrawler.com/. Results from various search engines are summarized in an easy to read form.

Mirror site is often set up with the purpose of backing up a popular site if it ever has problems—some times a mirror site will be used for load balancing, when a website becomes too busy the response times may slow down and a mirror site on a different server can be used to keep the service running as normal.

Misspellings People quite often spell words incorrectly when using search engines. Pages which use common misspellings will quite often receive extra hits, so it is a useful technique to include common misspellings of words in ALT tags, keywords, page names and titles. A similar effect occurs when spaces are missed out and words are accidentally joined together. Often, intelligent marketers will also optimize sites for misspellings in order to capture this sort of traffic.

Monitoring If your site is not accessible on the Web, then your potential visitors cannot see it and access your products and services. So the longer your site is down, the more money you lose. That is why it is so important to always know that your site is up and running and then to react immediately if something goes wrong. Monitoring helps you here. It checks the availability of your site and notifies you immediately if it goes down, or some of its services are unavailable.

Motivated visits If two or more pages are browsed during a visit, this will be counted in the Motivated Visits report. The ratio of visits when more than one page is viewed to all visits is a good sign of your site's attractiveness.

Multiple Titles It used to be possible to repeat the HTML title tag in the header section of a page several times to improve search engine positioning. Most search engines now detect this trick.

Navigation paths are sequences of pages that the visitor viewed from the moment she enters the site to the moment she leaves. From the marketing view, it is important to know the most common paths your visitors follow to get to the landing pages. You will learn which of the navigation paths are the most effective. The frequent exit patterns will show where your site is underperforming. You will see where to improve the content of your site to make your visitors' experience perfect.

Negative keywords allow you to eliminate searches that you know are not related to your message. If you add the negative keyword "–vacation" to your keyword "Hawaii climate" your ad will not appear when a user searches on "vacation Hawaii climate." Negative keywords should be used with caution, as they can eliminate a large portion of a desired audience if applied incorrectly.

New visitor is a person arriving at your site for the first time. New visitors are always unique, although they are not the same as unique visitors. The number of new visitors will always be smaller than the number of unique visitors, because a unique visitor is one arriving for the first time in the selected period (so the system may identify the visitor as unique in the current period but it also knows that he has been before).

ODP The Open Directory Project (http://dmoz.org/)

Off-The-Page Optimization In addition to on-page factors, search engines are increasingly using off-page factors to calculate relevance. This is because off-page factors are more difficult to manipulate artificially. The most important off-page factor is link popularity. Others include link text, link community

and click popularity. Off-page optimization involves ensuring that these elements are in place to boost relevance for the targeted terms.

OOP Over-Optimization Penalty

Open Directory Project is an undertaking run by thousands of volunteer editors. In theory, this is a very exciting and powerful way to organize the web. In practice, there have been some problems with the behaviour of some of the editors, which have caused some initial difficulty for the organizers. Initially known as NewHoo, the project is now part of Netscape (and therefore of AOL). See http://directory.mozilla.org.

Optimized Pages Unlike Gateway pages, they are pages optimized for targeted key phrases, but integrated with the main website. They contain content relevant to the user and maintain brand consistency with the rest of the site. Optimized pages can be viewed as pages of the web site which serve as landing points for users coming in from search engines.

Optimization is the process by whichchanges made to a web page to improve the positioning of that page with one or more search engines. It is a means of helping potential customers or visitors to find a web site. Optimization may involve design/layout changes, new text for the title tags, Meta tags, ALT attributes, headings and changes to the first 200-250 words of the main text. A large image map at the top of a page should be moved further down the page. Frames should be avoided (unless navigational links are also provided within the frames)

Organic listings On many search engines within the results pages there will be sites that have paid to be there as well as the one that have gotten there by their own merits. These free listings are also known as the organic listings.

Organic search listings are delivered from the search engine's main database and are not affected in any way by 'paid' for or 'sponsored' advertising activity. Also know as 'natural' or 'algorithmic' results. Organic search results should form the core of a search marketing strategy, complemented by paid search campaigns.

OSEO (Organic Search Engine Optimization) helps to construct a site that ranks high in search engines without spending large amounts of cash.

Outbound Link is a link from a page of your site to another site.

Paid inclusion guarantees presence on a search engine's results in exchange for payment, without any guarantee of how high the listing will appear. A paid inclusion appears to the user as an editorial listing rather than as a sponsored link. Pricing is typically based on a flat fee or index fee.

Paid placement is a guaranteed listing that appears next to search results, usually in relation to specified keywords. In response to recent Federal Trade Commission guidelines, many search engines clearly identify paid placements as "sponsored links" and run them separately from the editorial portion of the page. Paid placement programs are typically based on cost-per-click (CPC) or cost-per-thousand (CPM) pricing, and the cost is higher than paid inclusion ads. Also known as pay-for-placement.

Page Popularity is a measure of the number and quality of links to a particular page (inbound links). Many search engines (and most noticeably Infoseek) are increasingly using this number as part of the positioning process. The number and quality of inbound links is becoming as important as the optimisation of page content. A free service to measure page popularity can be found at http://www.linkpopularity.com.

Page Rank is a proprietary numerical score that is assigned by Google to every web page in their index. PR for each page is calculated by Google using a special mathematical algorithm, based on the number and quality (as determined by Google) of the inbound links to the page. PageRank a technical asset of Google, it is an exponential-based value that signifies importance of a webpage. The PR will display as a number out of 10 in a green bar of the Google Toolbar whenever you visit a website.

Page View is used in site statistics as a measure of pages viewed rather than server hits. Many server hits may be made to access a single page, causing many separate log file entries. Analysis software can determine that these server hits were generated when a visitor viewed a single page, and group them together to provide this more useful method of counting visitors. Every time a complete page displays, it counts as one page view, even when the visitor just refreshes the page, or leaves it for a second and then comes back. This is a much more accurate metric than a hit for analyzing user experience.

PageRank for Money refers to selling or buying a link from a web page with a high Google PageRank for the stated purpose of increasing the other page's PR. This is highly frowned upon by Google and will result in a penalty for both pages if Google finds out about it.

Pay-per-Click is a type of search marketing where advertisers pay a set amount every time their ad is clicked by a prospect (otherwise known as a click thru). Some search engines, such as Overture, specialize in this type of advertising medium, although pay per click is not limited solely to pay-per-click engines. For instance, Looksmart, a directory, recently changed its business model to pay per click. Also, XML trusted feeds through Inktomi and Fast are sold at a per-click basis.

Pay-for-Inclusion services are designed for Webmasters that are having trouble getting pages listed in spider-based search engines. A main benefit of PFI is fast respidering (every 48 hours or so), giving site owners and Webmasters instant positioning feedback and the ability to change content frequently. Also, site owners can submit deep-linked pages and be guaranteed that the URL will be included. The typical PFI program is an annual URL-based subscription with regular refresh cycles and click-based reporting. These programs are highly effective and potent for use in conjunction with seasonal campaign pages.

Penalty is a punishment levied against a web page by a search engine as a result of using an SEO tactic that it doesn't approve of. Tactics that most often result in penalties include using hidden text, sneaky redirects, and linking to a bad neighborhood. A penalty usually results in a web page being credited for a lower Google PageRank (PR) than it has actually "earned". Penalties also result in a page being "buried" deep within the SERPS where it will almost never be found again by searchers.

PFI (Pay for Inclusion) Used by various search engines that guarantees that your site will be listed in a search engine database. Google is a noteable exception that does not 'offer' such a service.

Pop-up ad appears in a separate window above or beneath the user's current page. A pop-under ad is concealed until the top window is closed, moved, resized, or minimized. A pop-up ad is similar to a daughter window, but without an associated banner.

Portal is a web page that works as a starting point for a user's session on the Internet. Portals typically include a directory of websites, access to web services and shopping sites, and search functionality powered by a search engine provider. Examples of portals are AOL, Netscape, Yahoo, CompuServe, and EarthLink.

Portal Site is a generic term for any site which provides an entry point to the internet for a significant number of users. Examples are search engines, directories, built-in default browser or service provider homepages, sites hardwired to browser buttons, sites offering free homepages, email or personalised news and any popular (or heavily advertised) sites that significant numbers of people may bookmark or set as default pages.

Position is the ranking assigned by a search engine to a page. The position denotes where that page is displayed in the search results for a given keyword or phrase.

Positioning Technique a method of modifying a web page so that search engines (or a particular search engine) treat the page as more relevant to a particular query (or a set of queries)

Positioning is the process of ordering web sites or web pages by a search engine or a directory so that the most relevant sites appear first in the search results for a particular query. Software such as PositionAgent, Rank This and Webposition can be used to determine how a URL is positioned for a particular search engine when using a particular search phrase. The

GoHip Search site allows you to see positioning information from many of the big search engines, displayed all on one page.

PPC Pay-per-Click.

PR (PageRank) is Google's proprietary measure of link popularity for web pages. Google offers a PR viewer on their Toolbar.

Query is a request for information, usually to a search engine or a database. The user types in words or topics, and the search engine returns matching results from its database. A query is at the center of every search engine interaction.

Ranking is the order a search engine shows results extracted from its database, relevant to the searcher's query. Each search engine uses its own unique algorithm to rank pages. Most major search engines use the ranking algorithms that combine both keyword relevance and page popularity.

Reach is the total number of unique users who will be served your ad over a specific period of time. Reach is often expressed as a percent of the universe for the demographic category. Also known as an unduplicated audience.

Reciprocal Links to another website placed on your site in exchange for links back to your site from theirs. This is a proven way to build link popularity, which is instrumental in getting high search engine rankings. Reciprocal links improve the link popularity of sites, webmasters exchange links, so when one site places a link to another site in exchange for the other site doing the same in return, this is reciprocal linking. Link exchange is a good strategy for low-budget sites, however you should take a close look at the site you are going to link to, because a search engine can penalize your site for reciprocal linking if the site has been blacklisted by the search engine.

Redirects When a server tells a browser to load another page instead of that requested it is called a redirect. Redirects are started in different ways. Auditor analyzes redirect URLs if they result from server responses 3xx, and Meta refresh. To turn the check on or off, you should open 'Check Rules' in 'Options' on the 'Scan' button menu.

Referral fees are paid in exchange for delivering a qualified sales lead or purchase inquiry. For example, an affiliate drives traffic to other companies' sites, typically in exchange for a percentage of sales or flat referral fee.

Registration is the process of informing a search engine or directory that a new web page or web site should be indexed.

Relevancy Algorithm is the method used by search engines and directories to match the keywords in a query with the content of all the Web pages in their database so the Web pages found can be suitably ranked in the query results. Each search engine and directory uses a different algorithm and frequently changes this formula to improve relevancy.

.**Repeat visits** are users who browsed your site more than once during the selected time period. In other words, these are all visits minus the first visits (or unique visitors) in the selected period. The percentage of repeat visits to all visits will give you a good picture of how appealing the content of your Web site is.

Re-submission is repeating the search engine registration process one or more times for the same page or Website. This is regarded with suspicion by search engines because it can be indicative of spamming techniques. Some search engines will de-list sites for repeated re-submission. Others limit the number of submissions of the same page in a 24 hour period. Occasional re-submission of changed pages is usually not a problem.

RFP Request for Proposal.

Robot is a program that runs automatically without human intervention. A robot is typically endowed with some artificial intelligence, so it can adjust to the various situations it may encounter. Two common types of robots are agents and spiders. Also known as a bot.

ROBOTS Tag Meta information tag used to tell visiting search engine robots how to behave (e.g. not to index a certain page, or not to archive a certain page)

Return on investment (ROI) is the benefit gained in return for the cost of your ad campaign. Although exact measurement is nearly impossible, your clickthrough rate and your conversion rate combined with your advertising costs can help you assess the ROI of your campaign.

RSS Feeds is an acronym for Rich Site Summary or Rich Site Syndication. RSS feeds use an XML document to publish news headlines. This document is submitted to sites which may choose to display the information in their site or program which uses an aggregator to parse the information.

SE Search engine

Search Engine is a searchable online database of internet resources. It has several components: search engine software, spider software, an index (database) and a relevancy algorithm (rules for ranking). The search engine software consists of a server or a collection of servers dedicated to indexing Internet Web pages, storing the results and returning lists of pages to match user queries. The spidering software constantly crawls the Web collecting Web page data for the index. The index is a database for storing the data. The relevancy algorithm determines how to rank queries. Examples of major search engines are Google, AOL, MSN and Lycos, etc.. Examples of major directories are Yahoo!, LookSmart and ODP.

Search Engine Friendly refers to a web page that has been designed and optimized for high search engine rankings. A search engine friendly page also makes it easy for search engines to follow the links on the page.

Search Engine Optimization (SEO) is the process of optimizing a website or web page to increase its visibility within the search engine results. Search engine optimization entails making sure that there is content relevant to the targeted key phrases on the web site, and that search engine spiders can find this content easily. Good search engine optimisation will ensure that this content is also useful to the user. Without relevant content, SEO techniques can only be partially successful, and will probably stray into the wrong side of search engine Acceptable Use Policies. See also 'ranking algorithms.'

Search engine optimization writing is specialized copywriting that entails weaving keywords and keyphrases into marketing or informational copy. The purpose of search engine optimization copywriting is to gain prime positioning for the desired keyphrases, as well as increase page conversion rates.

Search Engine Positioning, also known as Search Engine Optimisation (SEO), is a phrase to describe the practice of positioning a web site within the search engine results. A multitude of techniques are involved in successful search engine positioning. Not only must a web site be optimised, but it's link popularity must also be built. Good visibility in directories must be gained and other search engine marketing techniques pursued, such as Pay-per-Click campaigns. Search engine positioning has evolved over the last few years. While initially involving only search engine optimization, the industry has grown to include a whole array of additional techniques.

Search Engine Results Pages (SERPS) is the ranked listing of web pages that are returned for a specific search query.

Search Engine Spider searches engines, and other sites send robots (also known as spiders, bots, and crawlers) to read and index your site's pages. A search engine spider is an automated software program designed to find and collect data from Web pages. This is included in a search engine's index. It follows links to find new pages on the Web. Traces of a spider's activity can be found in server logs. You can see which files they requested. Search engine spiders identify themselves when they visit a site, for example, Google's spider is Googlebot, Yahoo!'s spider name is Yahoo! Slurp.

Search engine submission is the process by which one makes search engines aware that ones website is ready to be indexed by the search engine spiders. In general search engines spider the web on a regular basis, and will eventually find your web site by following a link from a site already within its index. It is sometimes necessary however to manually submit a new site which has not been linked, or to use a paid for inclusion process to ensure quick inclusion into the database. The search engine submission process involves going to a specified section of the search engine web site (the "Add URL" page) and inputting details which can include those web pages that one requires to be spidered. The term 'submission' also covers the process of requesting a listing in the directories.

Search optimization tactics and techniques that make it easier for spiders to find your page, contributing to higher ranking on a list of search engine results. Basic optimization starts with listing relevant keywords in your metatags and building clear and descriptive words into page copy, title, text hyperlinks and image file names. It's also important to design your site in a logical link structure and follow standard HTML conventions, avoiding the use of frames, dynamic URLs, Image Maps and JavaScript for navigation.

Search Query refers to the keyword, keyphrase, or list of words that you type into a search engine to find web pages on a topic that you're interested in.

Search Term is the word or phrase entered by a user into a search engine in order to perform a search. The search engine or directory then uses its algorithm to search its database of pages or sites to find a matching key phrase and return a list of results. Users may enter general search terms, such as "insurance", or they may enter more focused terms, such as "UK insurance brokers". A properly focused search term set forms the core of a good search engine positioning strategy and it is important to ensure that these are reflected in the actual content on the website. A search engine promotion that targets popular but relevant search terms has the advantage of driving targeted traffic, which can result in high conversion rates. Gaining knowledge of the general trends and habits of searchers, and having experience of the complexities of search term selection, can make the difference between search engine promotion failure and success.

SEM Search Engine Marketing

SEMPO Search Engine Marketing Professional Organization

SEO is the abbreviation for 'Search Engine Optimization'. SEO is normally used to describe the process of manipulating a website's pages in order for them to rank higher in search engine indices. Successful SEO can result in a site, which features prominently in a major search engine such as Google or MSN, delivering a significant amount of new visitors. SEO can contribute to the overall success of your website marketing. The process of SEO can involve changing a web page's content and html code so that a search engine 'spider' can find specific information more easily. Additionally, SEO occasionally involves the re-coding of a websites linking architecture. SEO combined with a set of targeted 'Key Phrases' (search terms people are using in search engines) can result in your website gaining high positioning for your most popular products or services. Furthermore, SEO can help target users focused to your area of expertise, enhancing user experience and eliminating excess unwanted click-throughs. SEO is a key element in the online marketing of a website as it can help potential visitors find the information they are searching for before discovering a competitor's site. SEO can also be known as 'Search Engine Positioning' or SEOR 'Search Engine Optimisation & Registration'.

Share of voice is a relative portion of inventory available to a single advertiser within a defined market sector over a specified time period.

Site Depth refers to the number of pages contained within a web site. Sites with more depth have a higher number of pages.

Site Map is a web page that links to all pages found on your website in an intelligent and coherent manner. Such a page is excellent resource for getting a search engine to spider all pages found within a website.

Site Submission this is the actual process by which a site is directly submitted to a search engine for inclusion into their database. Some search engines charge a certain amount for 'guaranteed inclusion' into their search index.

Skyscraper is a tall, thin ad unit that runs down the side of a web page. A skyscraper can be 120 x 600 pixels or 160 x 600 pixels.

Spam is any search engine optimisation method a search engine deems to be unethical. Some people say that Spam is word made up by the search engines to cover up their inability to detect sites using tactics they are unhappy with.

Spidering search engine is one that uses machines to fetch Websites and record its pages. The database of over 2 billion Web pages in Google's search index was gathered together using Google machines and GoogleBot (Google's so-called "spider" or Web crawler technology).

Splash Page While being similar to a doorway page, the purpose of a splash page is more artistic—a grand entry way to a website. The use of a splash page is poor design and not good for proper search engine optimization.

SQL Structured Query Language

Stemming is a function of some search engines and directories which allows results to be returned from some or all keywords based on the same stem as the keyword entered as a search term. For example, when stemming is switched on, a search for the word dance will return matches for any word whose stem is danc-, matching the keywords dance, dancer and dancing

Stop Word is a word which is ignored in a query because the word is so commonly used that it makes no contribution to relevancy. Examples are common net words such as computer and web, and general words like get, I, me, the, etc.

Submission is a process of entering a URL and other information about a site in a special form and submitting this form to a search engine so it includes your site in its index. In the early stages of Web building, submission to a search engine was the only way of telling them about a site's existence, and getting them to visit and register it. New technologies made it possible for the search engines to crawl the Web regularly, and, as a result, cross-linking of the Web sites became a more important factor for a site's inclusion. There are several small search engines having crawlers with limited functionality. These search engines do not regularly spider the Web. They accept submissions as their primary method of inclusion of new sites. These are the majority of search engines in our auto-submission section. If you want traffic from these search engines, you should submit to them. There are two main questions that need answering when talking about submissions: 1) how many pages you need to submit and 2) how often you will need to resubmit. We recommend that you submit only the main page to a directory and a few most important and keyword-optimized pages to a search engine. You do not need to resubmit pages unless you are sure they were not indexed after the first submission. If you have made important changes to the some of the pages' content, you can resubmit these pages.

Submission service is any agent which submits your site to many search engines and directories. Useful to get listed with many of the minor search engines, but don't rely on such services to get listed with the major search engines. Many of these services are automatic and run from web sites. Others run off line. Some are free. Beware of supplying your email address to the so called FFA (free for all) services—you may receive lots of spam.

Submissions are the act of submitting your site to the add URL page on a search engine. Also the act of submitting your site to a directory.

Submitting Your URLs is is the process of telling a search engine or directory about your web pages. The URLs that you submit are placed into a queue for later crawling or human review. If you have backlinks pointing to your web pages, there is usually no need to submit your URLs to the search engines because their crawlers will find the pages on their own and index them. You do need to submit your URLs to directories however because they use humans instead of robots to visit the sites that you submit and evaluate them.

Syndication is an option that allows you to extend your reach by distributing ads to additional partner sites.

Target audience refers to the intended audience for an ad, usually defined in terms of specific demographics (age, income, etc.), product purchase behavior, product usage, or media usage.

Targeted traffic references visitors to your web site that are interested in your particular product or service.

Text ad is designed for text delivery, with concise, action-oriented copy and a link to your website. Because they are not accompanied by graphics, text links are easy to create and improve page download time. Also known as a sponsored link.

Text optimization is the process of constructing a website page that will be seen by search engines specifically to promote the relevancy of a certain key phrase. Good text optimisation should not utilize random key phrases, but should maximize the value of existing content, such as specific informational topics or product information.

Timeouts indicate the number your server failed to respond. This includes all the timeouts recorded by all the Site Monitoring tests within the selected period.

Title tag is at the top of this webpage indicated by the words "Title tag—SEO Glossary." Search engines pay special attention to this tag as it is the first thing seen by spiders in the code. In the results pages it is also the link text that you click on, it is important to have the titles descriptive to the individual page.

Title is the text contained between the start and end HTML tags of the same name. This text is associated with (but not displayed in) the web page containing these tags, and is displayed in a special position (usually at the top of the window) by the web browser. Title text is important because it normally forms the link to the page from the search engine listings, and because the search engines pay special attention to the title text when indexing the page. Don't confuse this text with heading text within the web page which often looks like the title. Usually this will be rendered either using the HTML heading tags or just rendered with a large font size.

Titles with keyword indicate how many web pages have your keyword in their titles. It helps you estimate how many web pages have been optimized for your target keyword because Titles are very important for SEO. If the number of optimized Titles is low compared with the competition, this is a great advantage.

Token is a tracer or tag attached by the receiving server to the address (URL) of a page requested by a user. A token lasts only through a continuous series of requests by a user, regardless of the length of the interval between requests. Tokens can be used to count unique users.

Top 10 Ranking is a web page that is listed in the first 10 search results for a search query. Top-10 in Google also means on the first page using the standard search criteria

Traffic is the term used to describe the amount of visitors that view web pages. When talking to an SEO company they will often use terms such as targeted traffic and qualified traffic—this is the art of attracting visitors to your site who have an interest in the site's theme.

Traffic sites are sites built solely with the purpose of obtaining rankings in search engines. They generally consist of nothing but doorway pages and are designed to snare search engine traffic and pass it on to the main web site. Unscrupulous search engine optimisers often use many traffic sites which are extensively cross-linked to manipulate link popularity. This technique is also known as 'domain spamming' and is forbidden by all search engine terms of use. The use of this technique is a sure way of earning a ban from the index. Google is growing increasingly adept at identifying clusters of traffic sites which use this technique to hoard link popularity, and removing them from its index.

Unique user is a single individual or browser who accesses a site or is served unique content and/or ads. Unique users can be identified by user registration or cookies. Also known as a unique visitor.

Unique visitor is a person who accesses a web site. Web servers record the IP addresses of each visitor, and this is used to determine the number of real people who have visited a web site. If for example, someone visits twenty pages within a web site, the server will count only one unique visitor (because the page accesses are all associated with the same IP address) but twenty page accesses.

Universe is the total population of the audience you're measuring.

Uptime shows the server uptime (by percentage). Uptime is the percentage of time your server was reachable during a selected period.

URL is short for Uniform Resource Locator. This is an address used to specify a unique Internet resource. The beginning of the address points to the type of resource or scheme, for example http: for Web pages, ftp: for file transfers, telnet: for computer login sessions or mailto: for e-mail addresses. File URLs contain information on the method of access (scheme), the server accessed and the path of a file.

Usability Quite simply, usability is making your site easy for your customers to find the exact information they need when they need it. Anything that makes the process slower (like Flash animation served to a dial-up customer) inhibits usability. Conversely, easy, intuitive navigation and strong, informative text enhance usability.

Visit is a single session starting the moment a visitor enters your site to the moment she leaves. For example, if the report tells you had 2,600 visits on a certain day, it means the users came to your Web site 2,600 times. More technically, a visit is a sequence of requests during a session, all made by the same visitor identified by a cookie file (or IP address, user agent and other browser settings that can help to recognize the visitor). The session begins when the visitor moves to your Web page from a page located at a different domain—i.e. the referrer is an external Web page—and ends when the visitor leaves your Web page for another external Web page. There is no time limit for the session continuing if the external referrer is identified. Sometimes, the external referrer is not defined. This often happens when a visitor's firewall or special software program cloaks referrer information. So, if the referrer is unknown, such a visitor's session is considered new after 15 minutes inactivity. A visitor may come to your site several times a day. All these will count as visits, whereas only his first visit during the day (or other selected period of time) is included in the 'Visitors' number.

Vortal Site is site built around one theme or subject.

W3 World Wide Web

W3C World Wide Web Consortium

Web Copywriting the writing of text especially for a web page. Similar to the writing of copy for any other type of publication, good web copywriting can have a great effect on search engine positioning, so it forms a major part of optimization.

Web Page is a single document on the World Wide Web specified by a unique address or URL and that may contain text, hyperlinks, and graphics. A Web page is a part of a group of hypertext documents that form a Web site. Web pages are usually created with HTML (Hypertext Markup Language). The Web page is returned by the server in response to the URL request.

XHTML Extensible Hypertext Markup Language

XML Extensible Markup Language (file.xml)

www.ingramcontent.com/pod-product-compliance
Lightning Source LLC
Chambersburg PA
CBHW051233050326
40689CB00007B/907